THE BODY OF WRITING

The Body of Writing

AN EROTICS OF
CONTEMPORARY AMERICAN FICTION

Flore Chevaillier

THE OHIO STATE UNIVERSITY PRESS
COLUMBUS

Copyright © 2013 by The Ohio State University.
All rights reserved.

Library of Congress Cataloging-in-Publication Data
Chevaillier, Flore, 1979–
The body of writing : an erotics of contemporary American fiction / Flore Chevaillier.
p. cm.
Includes bibliographical references and index.
ISBN 978-0-8142-1217-2 (cloth : alk. paper) — ISBN 0-8142-1217-4 (cloth : alk. paper) — ISBN 978-0-8142-9318-8 (cd)
1. Semiotics and literature. 2. American fiction—History and criticism—Theory, etc. 3. English language—Style. 4. Reading. I. Title.
PN98.S46C48 2013
813'.609—dc23
2012041520

Cover design by Laurence J. Nozik
Type set in Adobe Sabon
Text design by Juliet Williams
Printed by Thomson-Shore, Inc.

∞ The paper used in this publication meets the minimum requirements of the American National Standard for Information Sciences—Permanence of Paper for Printed Library Materials. ZNSI Z39.48–1992.

9 8 7 6 5 4 3 2 1

c o n t e n t s

illustrations

acknowledgments

The body of this book has been shaped by the generous contributions of mentors, professors, colleagues, friends, and family. First, I am deeply grateful to R. M. Berry for his guidance on my dissertation, which was the foundation for this book. His insight, wisdom, and encouragement before, during, and after the completion of this project have been essential to my life as a writer and scholar. I also owe many thanks to Antoine Cazé, my co-director at the Université d'Orléans, who inspired me to study and write about adventurous works of literature. I am most grateful for his time, direction, and support over the course of my undergraduate and graduate studies. Andrew Epstein, S. E. Gontarski, Lauren Weingarden, Christopher Shinn, Mathieu Duplay, François Happe, and Claire Maniez offered valuable feedback in the early stages of this project.

The Julia Burnett Bryant Memorial Award and research grants from Florida State University subsidized my research and allowed me to conduct interviews with Joseph McElroy, Carole Maso, and Steve Tomasula. I thank each of them for allowing me to use our conversations in this book. Many thanks to Carole Maso for eye-opening discussions and for her enthusiasm for my work. I owe a special debt of gratitude to Steve Tomasula for his profound generosity and continued support of this project, as well as for his invigorating correspondence and conversations. I also thank him for many references indispensable to the evolution of this project. Last, but certainly not least, through the years, Joseph McElroy has had invaluable influence on my critical sensibilities; without him and his friendship, what follows would have been a lesser book. I am forever grateful for his stimulating conversations, generous correspondence, and subtle insights at so many steps along the way.

I am very appreciative of two anonymous readers' perceptive comments on my manuscript; their astute responses and reading suggestions have sharpened the contours of my argument. I would also like to express my appreciation to Sandy Crooms, Eugene O'Connor, Juliet Williams, Kristen Ebert-Wagner, Larry Nozik, Malcolm Litchfield, and Laurie Avery at The Ohio State University Press for their guidance and support. Eugene O'Connor and Juliet Williams tended, literally, to the body of my writing and made sure that it looked its best. I am also thankful to Sandy Croom's encouragement, patience, consideration, and expertise, which have made the process of publishing the book fulfilling at so many levels.

I am grateful to the Taylor & Francis and Rodopi presses for permission to reincorporate here revised versions of Chapter Two initially published as "Semiotics and Erotics in Joseph McElroy's *Plus*." *Critique. Studies in Contemporary Fiction* 50.3 (2009): 227–240, and Chapter Four initially published as "Erotics and Corporeality in Theresa Hak Kyung Cha's *DICTEE*." *Transnational Resistance: Experience and Experiment in Contemporary Women's Writing*. Eds. Stephenie Young and Adele Parker. Rodopi Press, 2013. I also thank Dalkey Archive Press, the Berkeley Art Museum, and Steve Tomasula for allowing me to reproduce pages of *AVA*, *DICTEE*, and *VAS*.

At various stages of this project, I relied on the help of friends and family, and I thank them for their support. I am especially grateful for the suggestions and encouragements of Rebecca Pennell, Joanna Beall, Matthew Hobson, Nick Allin, Tatia Jacobson Jordan, Jayson Iwen, Amy Hobbs-Harris, Simten Gurac, and Pierre Delacolonge. Special thanks to Bruno and Arlette, my parents, and Maud and Luc, my siblings, with whom I share a fascination with language. I thank each of them for countless contributions to the process of writing this book.

Finally, the person who has been the most centrally involved in the evolution of this project is Fabien Corbillon, to whom I owe the greatest thanks. I could not have written this book without his support, encouragement, wit, and affection. His belief in my ideas and endeavors has been a constant source of strength and inspiration. Loving thanks to Noah, who joined us in the last stages of this project and shared me with the day-to-day labor of writing this book. It is impossible for me to do justice to the joys that he has brought in our lives. I dedicate this book to them.

i n t r o d u c t i o n

The literary criticism of the past few decades has inclined toward an understanding of experimental literature in privative terms: innovative texts, in their linguistic experimentations, are perceived to negate social conventions. In this context, formally innovative writing is considered alternative, oppositional, defiant, subversive, transgressive, and resistant. Because authors such as William Gass, Raymond Federman, John Barth, Ronald Suckenik, Leslie Scalapino, Walter Abish, Ursula Le Guin, Robert Coover, Lydia Davis, Harry Mathews, Susan Sontag, and Clarence Major deconstruct literary traditions, they are understood to denounce and resist the ideological rules that shape literature and society. In a novel such as Thomas Pynchon's *Gravity's Rainbow,* the subversion of traditional elements of plot, character, and narrative voice opposes narrative closure, thereby undermining traditional reading practices. Salman Rushdie's *Satanic Verses*'s unstable, polyphonic, ironic, ambiguous, and self-contradictory narration disrupts dualistic thinking and attacks oppressive religious, imperialist, and nationalist discourses. Donald Barthelme's collage of urban vignettes, seemingly unrelated details, disembodied voices, and contradict-ing monologues rejects conventional divisions between high and low culture and breaks down established conceptions of fiction-writing. Kathy Acker's pastiche and cut-up techniques negate the phallocentric power structures of language and resist misogynistic capitalist society. While these accounts of formally innovative writing's goals and outcomes are accurate, they provide a primarily negative interpretation of it: texts are recognized as reactions to the hegemony, attacks on power, destruction of oppressive models, and so forth. This apprehension is valuable, as it clarifies the inherent politics of formal experiments. Yet, in focusing strictly on experimental texts' "rejec-tions," "attacks," or "oppositions," we stress what these texts respond to more than what they offer. In other words, the rhetoric of aesthetic negation does not do justice to the positive aesthetic liberation experienced in these works.

This rhetoric comes, in part, from writers' own description of their aims as transgressive and resistant. Sukenick argues that "it takes form to destroy form," thereby situating his alternative writing in negation of a literary tra-dition ("The New Tradition" 40). Barth's characterization of the "Literature of Exhaustion" positions his fiction in response to the "used up" literary tradition to be imitated and employed ironically. Federman insists that fic-tions should "question, challenge, undermine" "the traditional novel" "by a deliberate destruction and demystification of the well-made character," "by the elimination of plot," and "by the willful undermining and demys-tification of social reality" (*Surfiction* 310). Congruent with writers' views on the purpose of experimental fiction is its anthologization and critique. Philip Stevick's *Anti-Story: An Anthology of Experimental Fiction* classifies fictions in the following categories: "Against Mimesis," "Against 'Reality,'" "Against Event," "Against Subject," "Against the Middle Range of Expe-rience," "Against Analysis," "Against Meaning," and "Against Scale." In the critical arena, Linda Hutcheon explains the works of Barth and Coover as "attempts to explode realist narrative conventions" (*A Poetics* xii). Paul Maltby stresses that Barthelme, Coover, Pynchon, Burroughs, DeLillo, Acker, and Reed are "dissident" writers who "deconstruct the social codes" (21) and "subvert the rules by which language normally confers meaning" (186). Charles Russell has underlined that, because "all perception, cogni-tion, action, and articulation are shaped, if not determined, by the social domain," postmodern experimental fictions' "new aesthetic and social configuration[s]" transform prevailing paradigms (34). These accounts address important aspects of innovative fiction, but I suspect that their emphasis on its oppositional nature appeared, to some extent, in reaction to attacks on the relevance of experimental works, especially in the context of postmodern writing.

In the eighties and early nineties, critics have emphasized postmodernism's passivity, self-regarding tendencies, and overall political inefficacy. Andreas Huyssen, for instance, claims that the "American postmodernist avantgarde [. . .] is not only the endgame of avant-gardism. It also represents the fragmentation and the decline of the avantgarde as a genuinely critical and adversary culture" (170). Terry Eagleton stresses that postmodernism's "cultural relativism and moral conventionalism, its scepticism, pragmatism and localism, its distaste for ideas of solidarity and disciplined organization, its lack of any adequate theory of political agency: all these would tell heavily against it" (*Illusions* 134) In response to such views, critics have demonstrated that formally innovative fictions are examples of powerful political texts in the postmodern tradition. Departing from examinations of formal innovation as politically ineffective, these analyses of innovative writing have made clear the connection between linguistic experimentations and prevailing cultural systems. More specifically, they have elucidated the political involvement in formal experiments regarded as "a new kind of flatness or depthlessness, a new kind of superficiality in the most literal sense" (Jameson 9). While this elucidation was and still is necessary and valuable, it tends to overemphasize the negative politics of innovative works, which does not fully correspond to the research of recent innovative texts.

Criticism recently shifted toward a reassessment of formally innovative writing's positive inventions: Marcel Cornis-Pope has demonstrated that "Innovative fiction combines [. . .] a poetics of *resistance* with one of *reformulation,* highlighting the process of continuous rearticulation that the novel performs on life" (34–35). Because postmodern innovative writers recognize that the production of a "new reality" is never "autonomous" from "the ideological investment inherent in every narrative act," innovative "*reformulations*" are not dissociable from "their *resistance*" (Cornis-Pope 35). While Cornis-Pope elaborates on the reformulation and resistance of postmodern innovative fictions, I wish to examine the positive outcomes of the "*reformulations*" he highlights. Here, my goal is not to imply that experimental fictions are apolitical, but to point out that innovative writers and their critics, in an attempt to situate experimental writing's alternative strategies in a historical, political, and literary context, have overstressed the resistant, negative, and oppositional essence of innovation against its positive experience. I argue that fictions that have inherited from 1960s and 1970s literary experimentations offer pleasurable productions that are not merely at the service of oppositional political agenda. In other words, seeing these fictions within a political framework is right, but in celebrating them *only* as resistant to dominant powers, we fail to recognize their affirmative productions. In line with this claim and to avoid confusion with the negative aesthetic rhetoric associated with the terms "experimental" or "avant-garde," I have chosen instead the more neutral category, "formally innovative," to label the works of this study.

An affirmative engagement with literature is particularly striking in the novels studied in this book, as they offer sensual and pleasurable immediacy that does not rely strictly on a momentary evasion of dominant ideology, but fosters instead a political practice *through* ecstatic experiences. Hence, the rhetoric of dissidence and radicality accounts partially for the aesthetics of Joseph McElroy, Carole Maso, Theresa Hak Kyung Cha, and Steve Tomasula. In other words, *Plus* (1977), *AVA* (1993), *DICTEE* (1982), and *VAS* (2003) have affinities with some of the alternative writing strategies of Pynchon, Rushdie, and Acker; however, the oppositional discourse developed to examine these works is not sufficient to address the sensual ways in which McElroy, Maso, Cha, and Tomasula bring the unacknowledged physicality and the sensual surface of books into the experience of reading.[1] The bliss of making and interacting with these novels has outstripped the critical focus on the "dissident," "explosive," and "anti-realist" qualities of formally innovative texts.

To examine the pleasurable realm of these fictions, I propose an erotics of language, an embodied interpretive methodology that emphasizes the link between linguistic structures and the body. My interest in this methodology is influenced by Susan Sontag's essay "Against Interpretation," which condemns the practice of interpretation of works of art, claiming that the interpreter provides another text that nonetheless fails to render what the work of art really *is*. For Sontag, interpretation misses the "pure, untranslatable, sensuous immediacy" of art (9). Instead, Sontag proposes to avoid the overemphasized focus on the content of a work by stressing form *and* content, which forces readers and viewers to consider their sensory experience. She

---

1. There has been a debate about the spelling of the title of Cha's book. Following Juliana Spahr, I will capitalize *DICTEE* when I refer to it but keep other critics' usage when I quote them. Cha's title allows a pun on the noun dictation, the act of dictating, and the feminine past participle of the verb, the dictation of a feminine entity. The use of upper-case (the accent is not necessary when a French word appears in upper-case) allows an additional interpretation of the word. In the upper case title, it is unclear whether the accent is accidentally missing, which would be erroneous. Because Cha plays with voluntary "errors" in her use of French and English throughout her text, the use of *DICTEE* appropriately reflects the multiple layers and uncertainty of her language.

concludes that "In place of a hermeneutics we need an erotics of art" (14), a call this book takes up. Elaborating an erotics of recent innovative literature implies that we engage in the formal pleasure of its experimentations with signifying techniques and with the materiality of their medium—image, print, sound, page, orthography, and syntax. The enjoyment of these experimentations does not lead us away from the practical and political outcomes of literature; they are in fact political forms of expressions. Thus, an erotics of innovative fictions highlights these works' positive ideas and affects best understood in analogy with erotic experiences.

"Erotic" refers here not to sexual arousal but to the "intellectual stimulation associated with the brief and unexpected flash of the forbidden, to the sexuality of language," or as Patrick Fuery puts it, to a "critical moment [. . . that is also] a point of ecstasy in which the idea has orgasmic force" (Ott "(Re)locating" 207; Fuery 6). These ecstatic moments will occur when language seems radically excessive. DeKoven clarifies this use of linguistic practices in her definition of experimental writing as "erotic in its excess: the unassimilable excess of meaning, or of repetition, or of sound play, or of surprise. With his '*jouissance de la texte*,' [*sic*] his literary 'physics of bliss,' Barthes formulates dramatically the value to the reader of the alternative experience experimental writing provides" (16). This excess cannot be contained within a traditional production of meaning, and so the reader feels a loss of control. Just like during the erotic experience when eroticism is in excess of any purpose, textual bliss surpasses any use of language for a specific end.

To elaborate on this textual bliss, I explore *Plus, AVA, DICTEE,* and *VAS* in relation to theories of eroticism and sensuality. I am informed by Georges Bataille, Julia Kristeva, Roland Barthes, Jean-Jacques Lecercle, Gilles Deleuze, Félix Guattari, and Hélène Cixous, whose works offer seminal studies of the intersection between literature, sexuality, and politics. In these theories, blissful writing and reading experiences occur in the linguistic elements of texts—sounds, rhythms, syntax, diction, and orthography. Their clarification of the erotic drive of linguistic forms is central to this project and to the understanding of McElroy's, Maso's, Cha's, and Tomasula's research in modes of writing that invite the body into the reading and interpretive realm. In fact, these writers are in dialogue with and have self-consciously extended the connections between their fictions and theories of the Semiotic, *jouissance*, libidinal drives, *écriture féminine*, and délire.

However, McElroy, Maso, Cha, and Tomasula also engage the material of their fictions in ways that are not accounted for in studies of eroticism. More specifically, although words, sentence structures, and sonorities are important to the experience of *Plus, AVA, DICTEE,* and *VAS,* their erotic materiality is best understood in connection with their visuality. *Plus* plays with different typefaces to illuminate power dynamics: the narration focusing on the main character, Imp Plus, is presented in lower case. The upper case is used for dialogue. *AVA's* appearance is often described as unusual and poetry-like since it combines fragments of sentences separated by blanks. *DICTEE* is a collage of texts that plays with pagination and typographical blanks; it also inserts photography, handwritten texts, and charts. *VAS,* the result of the collaboration between designer Stephen Farrell and writer Tomasula, presents a mixed-media product combining comic-comic strips, charts, documents, and illustrations on genetics and eugenics. To account for the typographic signification of these texts, I turn to Johanna Drucker's work on the visual form of the page. I also draw on the theories of visual arts critic Georges Didi-Huberman and film critic Laura Marks, as they elucidate textures and excesses in paint and film akin to the typographical and visual experimentations of the fictions studied here. As Katherine Hayles claims, "Literary texts, like us, have bodies, an actuality necessitating that their materialities and meanings are deeply interwoven into each other" (*Writing Machines* 107). In exploring the body of *Plus, AVA, DICTEE,* and *VAS,* I tie matters of the sensual and erotic to the material realities of texts.

This double methodology is in line with the historical situations of *Plus, AVA, DICTEE,* and *VAS,* whose linguistic and material explorations have apparent precedents in texts concerned with linguistic and paginal experiments, such as Stéphane Mallarmé's "Un coup de dés"and William Gass's *Willie Masters' Lonesome Wife.* Mallarmé's typographical explorations reveal that books are not just carriers of information, and Gass's novel shows that the typography of books is not incidental: his dramatic use of the textual materials positions the reader as a voyeur who must look at the sexually charged page. *Willie Masters' Lonesome Wife's* voyeuristic framework is in accord with the overall metaphor of writing and reading as sexual activities, which anticipates the sensual materiality of McElroy, Maso, Cha, and Tomasula's novels. As I will show, *Plus, AVA, DICTEE,* and *VAS* continue this tradition and respond to past material explorations in American literature, including Federman's *Double or Nothing* and *Take It or Leave It;* Suckenik's *Out, Mosaic Man,* and *Long Talking Bad Conditions Blues;* Gilbert Sorrentino's *Mulligan Stew;* Lee Siegel's *Love in a Dead Language;* and Abish's *Alphabetical Africa.* Federman, in particular, is famous for his commentaries on the significance of the page, and his views illuminate the typographical experiments of the novels studied here:

The very act of reading a book, starting at the top of the first page, and moving from left to right, top to bottom, page after page to the end in a consecutive prearranged manner has become *boring* and *restrictive*. [. . .] Therefore, the whole traditional, conventional, fixed, and boring method of reading a book must be questioned, challenged, demolished. [. . .] [T]he space itself in which writing takes place must be changed. That space, the page (and the book made of pages), must acquire new dimensions, new shapes, new relations in order to accommodate the new writing. (*Surfiction* 9–10)

Sukenick notes that when reading such reconfigured pages, the reader "is forced to recognize the reality of the reading situation [. . .], instead of allowing him to escape the truth of his own life" (*In Form* 25). Postmodern Avant-Garde literature "keeps returning" the reader to "his own life," but "one hopes, with his own imagination activated and revitalized" (*In Form* 25).

While *Plus, AVA, DICTEE,* and *VAS* are in keeping with the tradition of paginal and typographic experiments Federman and Sukenick explore, they also foreshadow New Media texts' investigations of our relationship with textual materials: in both kinds of texts the configuration of the words, letters, and "pages" is inextricable from meaning. Because McElroy's, Maso's, Cha's, and Tomasula's fictions call attention to the nature of books, to the relation between materiality and content, and to the rules that configure textual frameworks, they, much like New Media works, "can give us a deeper appreciation for the corollary propositions that media and materiality also matter" (Hayles *My Mother* 116). What's more, *Plus, AVA, DICTEE,* and *VAS* foreground an involvement of the body in reading processes, which invites us to consider "the importance of the book as a physical object and [. . .] criticism as material practice" (Hayles *Writing Machines* 19). As Hayles argues, the advancement of New Media texts has made this consideration even more apparent and timely. Electronic texts, such as Shelley Jackson's *Patchwork Girl,* call for bodily engagement in the fiction's content about monstrous bodies and texts, and for physical involvement via textual and digital strategies. In digital novels, the embodiment of reading, in line with the physical interactiveness of the electronic media, is not without recalling the embodied reading practices of *Plus, AVA, DICTEE,* and *VAS.* In that sense, the configuration of an erotic mode of writing and reading implies that New Media works grew not only from the exploration of technological possibilities in literature but also from the recognition of a positive political practice in our erotic engagement with texts, which Bataille, Kristeva, Barthes, Lecercle, Deleuze, Guattari, and Cixous inform. As in New Media, the form of the fictions examined here is their political potential: it enables sensuous interactions between reader and text, an interaction that leads us to reconsider the structures of the body and society. Consequently, as the chapters of this book progress and the questions of textual materiality and embodiment become more and more central, I concentrate on the New Media theories of Jay Bolter, Richard Grusin, Hayles, and Drucker's late work.

The Body of Writing draws from eclectic theories in response to the eclectic textual and material practices of *Plus, AVA, DICTEE,* and *VAS.* I have selected these texts because they provide insights on different aspects of the erotics of language, but they do not encompass the whole of its field. Each of these novels, however, is a powerful case study for building an erotics of language. The excess that calls for an erotic reaction to McElroy's, Maso's, Cha's, and Tomasula's fictions is evident in their juxtaposition of genres, techniques, materials, and voices. Lyn Hejinian addresses the "forces," "dynamics," and "motion[s]" (42) of such texts, which she qualifies as "open texts," or texts whose "elements [. . .] are maximally excited" (43) and whose "form is not a fixture but an activity" (47). Unlike closed texts that relay information in a single reading, open texts are "generative rather than directive" (43) and "situat[e] desire" (49) in language, not merely in what it expresses. Hejinian's description of open texts is valuable to this project, not only because McElroy's, Maso's, Cha's, and Tomasula's process-oriented, ambiguous, and displaced uses of language are "forces" that generate open texts' political potency but also because her insistence on "dynamics" and "motion" implies a bodily relationship with writing that involves "desire." This conception of texts, in engaging the corporeal, illuminates the reading of *Plus, AVA, DICTEE,* and *VAS*'s "radical *openness*" (Hejinian 42). The following chapters seek to establish the claim that these open texts' linguistic and paginal disruptions provoke an erotic examination of language and make possible a sensual and ultimately positive political experience of reading.

chapter one

Erotic Etudes

THEORY OF THE SELF AND LANGUAGE

In *Eroticism,* Bataille considers eroticism as a special form of sexuality. He claims that eroticism "leads to the discontinuity of beings, but brings into play their continuity" (13). Indeed, the sexual act requires that two beings interact intimately, which implies that, during this interaction, they lose their discontinuity: "Through the activity of organs in a flow of coalescence and renewal, like the ebb and flow of waves surging into one another, the self is dispossessed" (18). This loss of selfhood is crucial to the erotic experience, as "The whole erotic business of eroticism is to destroy the self-contained character of the participators as they are in their normal lives" (17). For Bataille, this violation of selfhood leads not only to the dissolution of the self but also to the social rules that create it. In other words, the erotic experience exists in relation to the transgression of a rule or a taboo, while it is also conditioned by its existence. Hence, "The experience of death in eroticism is, by definition, always only proximate—simultaneously rupturing and maintaining the limits of individual existence" (Sur-

9

kis 19).[1] For Bataille, both the erotic experience and the poetic experience rely on a questioning of the social rules forming the self, and on the loss of selfhood during this particular experience: "Poetry leads to the same as all forms of eroticism—to the blending and fusion of separate objects" (25). Although Bataille alludes to a possible connection between poetry and eroticism in this passage and mentions several literary works in his study, he does not explain in specific terms how "poetry leads to the same as all forms of eroticism."

Kristeva's theory of the Semiotic and the Symbolic clarifies the communion of the experience of language and bodily experience that arises through *jouissance*. The concept of *jouissance* originates with Jacques Lacan. For Lacan, *jouissance* involves libidinal pleasures from the Imaginary or prelinguistic structure of the subject, erupting in the Symbolic, the realm of culture, law, and language. *Jouissance* has the ability to disrupt this Symbolic order. In Kristeva's work, "*jouissance is not an object and does not have any object*," as it takes place when the separation between the self and its object blurs (*La révolution* 497).[2] Through this blurring of the self and the world, *jouissance* allows a multiplication of meaning.

In focusing on such linguistic phenomena, we can explore the repressed material at the origin of signifying processes. Indeed, according to Kristeva, language theorists have repressed the development that the body and the subject undergo during signifying processes. While Kristeva acknowledges that one must introduce a distance with respect to things in order to use language, language is not a pure mental abstraction for her. On the contrary,

---

1. While Bataille's exploration of eroticism in relation to sexual taboos, religion, murder, and beauty is valuable, feminist readers often criticize it because of its depiction of women's role during the erotic experience. Suzanne Guerlac notes that in *Eroticism* and *History of Eroticism*, the woman is an "object," "a prostitute"; "she is cast in the role of the already *aufgehoben* slave while the man enjoys the role of the master" (92, 94). As a matter of fact, in *Eroticism*, Bataille explains that "In the process of dissolution, the male partner has generally an active role, while the female partner is passive. The passive female side is essentially the one that is dissolved as a separate entity" (17). This distinction between masculine and feminine eroticism has been interpreted as sexist. Andrea Dworkin, for example, stresses that Bataille relies on a male-centered vision of sex. Judith Still, Susan Rubin Suleiman, and Susan Sontag ("Pornographic"), on the other hand, defend Bataille's theory against reproaches of sexism on the basis "that the relation [Bataille] highlights between sex and death is a *human* question" (Still 235). Like Still, Suleiman, and Sontag, I find it more relevant to focus on the human implications of Bataille's theoretical concepts, and I am interested, more specifically, in how they relate to literature.

2. The English version of *Revolution in Poetic Language* is a partial translation of Kristeva's project in French. In this study, the passages cited as *Revolution* refer to the English translation. The passages cited as *La révolution* are taken from portions of Kristeva's work not available in English translation. The translations of these passages are mine.

it exists as a product of the body. In emphasizing the importance of the body in linguistic constructions, Kristeva wants to avoid an understanding of art detached from the physical sensations that accompany its creation and reception. The relevance of Kristeva's theory to a study of erotics in contemporary texts relies on its inclusion of linguistic elements that have been, and often still are, overlooked in semiotics (i.e., the extralinguistic that is part of our experience of language). In that sense, her theory provides a framework to address processes of signification, not only in terms of sense-making but also in terms of kinetic rhythms, material expressions, and somatic productions. Because the writers analyzed in this study explore the relation between the body and language, theoretical models that respect this relationship, like Kristeva's, are key to our understanding of their works.

For Kristeva, bodily experiences of language occur through the interaction of the Symbolic and the Semiotic. The Symbolic relies on the regulations of rational discourse. The Semiotic is less tangible; it is the non-representational part of the signifying process located in the pre-oedipal phase of the child's development. At this stage, *pulsions*—energies that move through the infant's body—structure its life and articulate a mobile and ephemeral totality, which Kristeva calls the semiotic *chora*. She borrows the term *chora* from Plato's *Timaeus,* where it denotes "an essentially mobile and extremely provisional articulation constituted by movements and their ephemeral stases" (*Revolution* 25). Kristeva notes that the *chora*, which she associates with "rupture," "articulation," and "rhythm," "precedes evidence, verisimilitude, spatiality, and temporality" (*Revolution* 23, 26). Therefore, the *chora* does not signify: it is not a sign or a position, as it precedes language. The social construction that enables the subject to acknowledge the environment in which it evolves and to make statements about it is what Kristeva calls the "*thetic.*" In a non-*thetic* phase (i.e., in the *chora*), the subject has not yet developed an understanding of itself as a self—distinct from its object—and thus cannot use a linguistic structure that demonstrates this distinction. Hence, the semiotic *chora* becomes a pre-enunciation inseparable from the Symbolic, but in any signifying process, both the Symbolic and Semiotic poles are present; consequently, the subject cannot be exclusively symbolic or semiotic. As a result, the subject, or more specifically, the *sujet en procès,* is always in process or "always becoming" and "on trial," as it constantly balances semiotic and symbolic functions.

This is clear in *Plus,* for example, where a man's brain, called Imp Plus, is sent into orbit during a scientific experiment, "so the very brain, if it still was the brain, slid its canal beds—or, if he could have fixed himself at one point, seemed to slide and distribute its canal beds" (106). Imp Plus acts

not as a subject in the world but rather as an inclusive entity.[3] The trans-
formations of this entity challenge an understanding of a centered self. He
wonders, for example, if the solar panels used for the experiment are part of
himself: "They [the solar panels] were not inside of the brain. But they were
not inside the capsule, whose bulkheads were outside the brain or what
he had thought the brain [. . .]. The oblong cells on the panels might not
be the cells of Imp Plus, but they were part of what he was part of" (104).
Because Imp Plus does not know what is a part of him and what is inside or
outside of him, he inquires about the words that conceptualize his predica-
ment. This inquiry shows the limits of linguistic communication and slowly
challenges the symbolic order. He articulates: "Sockets was a word," and
"A question was what an answer was to" (1, 167). His sentences re-explore
the meaning of words such as "sockets" or "question," inquiring about
the ways in which we signify. Imp Plus explains that "in all the words that
passed was what they lacked. It was far more than the words were equal
to" (184). His questioning alludes to language's inclusion of both symbolic
and semiotic dimensions, its containment of precisely what, as symbolism, it
excludes. Such questioning recurs when Imp Plus expresses ambiguous and
polymorphous ideas. He says, for example, "A thing called laughter had
been graying or dampening or decaying a graph" (19). Unable to reduce
his expressions to a symbolic logic, Imp Plus assembles contradictory ideas:
laughter does not have colors, or wet textures. Hence, we see in Imp Plus's
language an example of the contradictions the Semiotic allows: how can
laughter be laughter if it has a color?

We understand, in Imp Plus's sentence, that the Semiotic invites us to
accept an unconceivable idea (i.e., that laughter has texture and color, and
that it can affect a graph). The seemingly incoherent statement introduces
polymorphous concepts: what a graying laughter is can be interpreted in
various ways. The word "dampening" itself carries the idea of "making
wet" or "depressing." Also, on a grammatical level, the repeating of "or"
enacts the constant change that resists the stability of the Symbolic. We realize here that, as Kristeva shows, the Semiotic can disrupt the narration: the
reader focuses not only on the message of Imp Plus's words but also on the
underlying substance that constructs language.

Because the text is strangely ambivalent, it draws attention to the morphemes that constitute it. In *Plus* and the other works explored in this

---

3. As a matter of fact, we are not sure how to refer to Imp Plus since, in the narration,
he is referred to as a "he," as he was formerly a man, but distinctions between "it" and "he"
are hard to draw because at first the character is deprived of his maleness, and then, as the
brain re-builds a body, "it" becomes a non-gendered being.

study, morphemes do not always respect their limits—they are not merely a function of signifying language—so that plays on sounds and meaning go beyond the standard uses of the linguistic code. Through these phonetic and semantic disruptions, the text brings us back to the "topography of the body which reproduces itself in them" (Kristeva "Phonetics" 34). This opening to the repressed *chora* allows a reacquisition of the libidinal energies at the root of language acquirement, which provokes the subject's *jouissance*. This re-emergence is revolutionary because "this semiotization sets off against social and linguistic norms a signifying practice in which the flux, the desire of the subject runs into language and disarticulates it by always maintaining it on the verge on being disintegrated by the drives" (Féral 10).[4] For Kristeva, avant-garde writing tries to bring the semiotic sublayer to the surface, making libidinous productions more visible. This conception of the avant-garde's balancing force against conventional ideologies has led critics to insist on the subversiveness of experimentations in innovative literature. However, what is often overlooked in Kristeva's treatment of the politics of the disruption of selfhood, which is also at the root of the erotic process, is its formation of a positive activity in texts. In other words, theories of the self and desire, such as Kristeva's, not only resist linguistic and social structures but also illuminate the pleasurable textual realities of text, which will be the focus of this study.

Analyses that dissociate the two complementary aspects of formally innovative writing—its subversive ventures and positive aesthetic productions—overlook what it offers beyond a response to the hegemony. The writing of Sukenick and Federman illuminates innovative writing's positive cultural function. Sukenick thinks of textual innovations as forms of "mutiny" that come from "a refusal to proceed as usual, a diversion of the channels of power to more constructive ends" (*Narralogues* 22). This "mutiny" defies traditional narrative models, while also offering alternate

---

4. The revolutionary impact of the Semiotic that Féral emphasizes in Kristeva's work is often debated: critics condemn Kristeva's indifference to historical and cultural difference. I suspect that this attack relies on the partial translation of *La Révolution du langage poétique*. The English version, which leaves out about two thirds of Kristeva's original dissertation, focuses solely on its first chapter, "Preliminary Theoretical Matters." The last two sections, "Semiotic Apparatus of Texts" and "The State and Mystery," deal with the ways in which the Semiotic, under the historical circumstances of the Third Republic (1875–1940) in France, works in Lautréamont's and Mallarmé's poetry. In these chapters, Kristeva is interested both in how political changes affect aesthetic productions and in how *géno-textes* may treat, at the literary level, questions of a given society that remain unanswered during a period of political turmoil. Ironically, the 1984 American translation of Kristeva's 1974 book emphasizes her theoretical apparatus, separating it from its practical applications, and Kristeva is now held responsible for her lack of concern for historical and cultural analyses.

linguistic practices. Therefore, Sukenick thinks of his work as an "unwriting" of "what has been formulated as experience," of traditional storytelling techniques, in order to create a "new sense of experience" ("Unwriting" 26). This "new sense of experience" is the positive production that tends to be overshadowed by the subversive narrative techniques of works such as *Mosaic Man*. For Federman, "New Fiction" fills "the linguistic gap created by the disarticulation of the official discourse in its relation with the individual" (*Critifiction* 25), but this "disarticulation" is inseparable from the liberation it provokes, a liberation that enables readers to "re-vision" literature and society (*Critifiction* 125). In *Plus, AVA, DICTEE,* and *VAS* the "new sense of experience" and "re-vision" occur not only in relation to our conceptual models but also in relation to our sensual involvement with these novels. By interacting with fictions that question dominant definitions of body and text, we are able to conceive alternative ways to interact with literature and with the world. As critics of experimental writing have pointed out, a reevaluation of aesthetic and social models takes place at the intellectual level, as we are forced to question ideologies. However, because of our erotic involvement with these open texts, we also engage in new aesthetic and social possibilities. In an erotic relationship with the text, we are not alienated from our bodies and can thus discover different prospects for political agency.

My emphasis on the relationship between body and language has affinities with Lecercle's exploration of "the abstraction of language from the human body, and the expression of the body in language" (111). For Lecercle, these expressions are marked in "*délire,*" or that which "is at the frontier between two languages, the embodiment of the contradiction between them" (44). These two languages are the abstract, systematic, and meaningful on the one hand, and the material, bodily, and self-contradictory on the other. Much like in Kristeva's model, these two languages coexist: subjects and texts are constituted dialectically, as the material is repressed and emerges in abstract language, thereby challenging it. *Délire* is a necessary part of language that "testifies to a disruption of discourse, and it is an attempt at reconstruction" (155). Thus, Lecercle's work focuses on the moments of hesitation in language, or in Kristeva's terms, the moments when the Semiotic tugs at the symbolic order: "*Délire* embodies the contradiction between the mastery of the subject and the re-emergence of chaos, of the original disruptive rejection" (43). A text that produces *délire* "dissolves the subject, threatens to engulf the reader in its disaster, yet saves him" (45). Lecercle proposes to explore this dissolution because our understanding of and relationship with language traditionally abstract the bodily from communication. Instead of eclipsing the organs that produce language from it, Lecercle pays attention to linguistic nontransparent uses that make language an expression of "the speaker's body, an outward expression of its drive" (44). According to him, *délire* is often part of fiction because both rely on "the mixture of danger and usefulness that words contain" (87). More specifically, flows of language in long sentences, unclear references of personal pronouns, unknown textual sources, humor, and obscure meanings are expressions of *délire*.

A text such as *DICTEE* epitomizes *délire*'s involvement of "language, nonsense, desire" (Lecercle 6). Cha's interest in sounds, patterns, repetitions, and fluxes stresses the "unsystematic," "self-contradictory," and "impossible" qualities of material language (Lecercle 44):

> Both times hollowing. Cavity. And germination.
> Both times. From death from sleep the appel. Both
> times appellant. Toward the movement. The move-
> ment itself. She returns to word. She returns to word,
> its silence. If only once. Once inside. Moving.

FIGURE 1. Theresa Hak Kyung Cha. *DICTEE* p. 151 (c) 2001 The Regents of the University of California. The University of California Press.

Here, Cha disrupts syntactical rules, mixes French and English, and uses repetitions and contradictions (see figure 1). She plays with short sentences to highlight the orderly basis of communication. At the same time, she accumulates fragmented phrases into incomplete sentences and ambiguous statements such as "She returns to word, its silence," which does not clarify how "word" and "silence" cohabitate: to what word should one return in order to reach silence?[5] And when does silence exist in words? In addition, "appellant" is a misspelled version of the French word "appelant," and the English word "movement" is close to the French word "mouvement." For Lecercle, such play on words follows basic phonetic development, while disrupting it when enabling each word to have more than one meaning. Cha's play on different sonorities—the nasal sounds in the French "appellant" which can also be applied to "movement" and the [s] repeated in the English words—calls our attention to the materiality of her text and shows that language comes

5. Throughout *DICTEE,* Cha uses misspellings and grammatical errors to express her position and that of other women when exiled and/or oppressed. Because inserting [*sic*] after each excerpt would be repetitive, I will remain faithful to the spelling of the text without mentioning its intentional "misspellings."

from "the depth of the body [. . .] where only affect and the passions of the body can be expressed" (Lecercle 35).

Cha's use of two languages also emphasizes the text's intermediary dimension and illustrates her own interstitial position. This interstice of language and culture reveals that, because *délire* concerns the relationship of language and the subject, it also concerns the concept of "frontier." When dealing with *délire,* "the problem of the establishment of frontiers becomes crucial[.] [I]t also means that language will always try to utter what cannot be said, the subject will always be tempted to go beyond the frontier: in order to define a boundary one must at least attempt to cross it. This is exactly what happens in *délire*" (51). In Cha's work, the negotiation of this frontier pertains not only to language and the subject but also to cultural borders. The pleasure readers take in sonic variations, paired with Cha's reflection on exile, racial stereotypes, patriarchal domination, and cultural struggles, makes a political statement in itself. In other words, the "constraints which are suspended in *délire,* as a result of which the subject dissolves," make the erotic—through the subject's dissolution—and the political inseparable (Lecercle 198). *DICTEE*'s politics lies in the renegotiation of the erotic and the national, but Lecercle shows that, because "libido is the energy of the collective unconscious, and *délire* is the direct product of libido," *délire* is essentially political (167).

Lecercle makes this claim based on Gilles Deleuze and Félix Guattari's account of social paradigms in *AntiOedipus* and *A Thousand Plateaus,* where the authors propose a nonlinear and nonhierarchical mode of organization, the "rhizome," which they oppose to the "arborescent" model of thought. Through the metaphor of the rhizome, Deleuze and Guattari point out the limits of the tree model rooted in a Cartesian capitalistic paradigm which is centered and fixed. They disapprove of the illusion of pre-traced destiny (i.e., divine, anagogic, historical, economic, structural, or hereditary) that lies in this model, and underline that it represses libidinous flows of energy. In resistance to the "arborescent" paradigm, the rhizome assembles different elements and resists a linear ordered growth within open systems, thus enabling the libidinal to become part of a Marxist resistance to capitalist powers. Because *délire* challenges frontiers, Lecercle writes, it offers "lines of flight" akin to the rhizomorphous modes of travel that de-center human energy away from linguistic stability and capitalist reproduction (198). In destabilizing the sedentary structures of exchange and representation, *délire* creates an alternative mode of expression and organization. In Deleuze and Guattari's work, much like in the studies of Kristeva and Lecercle, libidinal pleasures and political subversions are not distinguishable. Yet, interpretations of their works tend to emphasize the political to the detriment of the positive pleasurable production that accompanies and enables resistance.

Barthes's late work addresses more directly bliss's political upshot, as his analysis relies on an exploration of the readers' blissful experiences—what Barthes calls *jouissance*—in relation to a more reassuring, less disruptive experience of pleasure. Pleasure relies on the confirmation of one's cultural values and norms of interpretation, while *jouissance* relies on the violation of those norms and values. A text of *jouissance* presents the interaction of codes, a mix of languages, illogicality, incongruity, repetition, excess, and a dismantling of grammar and meaning. The reader of such texts is invited to "mi[x] every language, even those said to be incompatible" and "silently accep[t] every charge of illogicality, of incongruity" (*Pleasure* 3). The reader of *DICTEE* discovers that "the text no longer has the sentence for its model" but "a powerful gush of words, a ribbon of infra-language" (*Pleasure* 7):

From the back of her neck she releases her shoulders free. She swallows once more. (Once more. One more time would do.) In preparation. It augments. To such a pitch. Endless drone, refueling itself. Autonomous. Self-generating. Swallows with last efforts last wills against the pain that wishes it to speak.

FIGURE 2. Theresa Hak Kyung Cha. *DICTEE* p. 3 (c) 2001 The Regents of the University of California. The University of California Press.

Here, Cha disturbs grammatical rules in accumulating fragments and in using pronouns inadequately (see figure 2). In the phrase "the pains that wishes it to speak," the use of "it" is confusing because its referent is absent in the sentence. Since "it" should be omitted for the sentence to be correct grammatically, we become aware of the rules of linguistic constructions. In this passage, it feels as though words are "employed for their sensual texture, like printed papers in a collage, as well as for their textual value" (Drucker *The Visible* 147). Cha's use of the textual and sensual values of language insists on the power of radical changes that do not conform to rhetorical rules; her words are "unexpected, succulent in [their] newness [. . .] [—they] *glisten*, they are distracting, incongruous apparitions" (*Pleasure* 42).

For Barthes, these "incongruous apparitions" allow the reader to experience bliss, a state that challenges the self. "The dismantling of language is intersected by political assertion" because it does not conform to the linguistic rules that allow the subject to feel secure in a world whose "court, school, asylum, [and] polite conversation" rely on the logical structures of language (*Pleasure* 8, 3). But, as DeKoven reveals:

> We are not used to talking about linguistic structures as political. We generally restrict political analysis of literature to thematic content, or to those elements of style clearly related to it. We tend also to require, or feel uncomfortable without, evidence of conscious intention on the author's part, particularly for political, cultural analysis of a radical or avant-garde cast. (xx)

The kind of politics DeKoven write about relies on a debunking of the valorization of the conventional modes of signification in which the social subject is rooted, but it also engages, in *Plus, AVA, DICTEE,* and *VAS,* a pleasurable recovery. Thus, the reader of these texts, unlike the reader who remains in control and is pleased by the reassurances of his or her values, encounters the political force of *jouissance.*

This account of *jouissance* has, however, suffered a number of critiques: while Barthes's work on social and cultural myths is valued in the field of critical theory, his later work on the physical reactions to textual innovations has often been condemned. Jonathan Culler qualifies the "late Barthes" (from 1970 on) as "nostalgic or sentimental" for its "blend of knowingness and sentimentality" (439, 440). Culler, Eagleton, and other readers dismiss the shift from Barthes's analysis of dominant discourses to his later concern for the subject of that discourse. They also wish for the scientific rigor of the early Barthes and find the late Barthes too personal. Behind this second critique lies an assumption about which forms of writing are better for communicating about literature. But for Barthes, it would be illogical to elucidate the pleasures of art from a neutral and abstract viewpoint because the fragments used to elaborate on the text of *jouissance* are part of the message conveyed about the erotics of rupture. In talking about the dispersed self, Barthes must reflect the unorganized and nonintegrated environment through a resistance to coherence and hierarchical structure.

In addition to dismissing the form of Barthes's late works, Culler and Eagleton challenge his focus on a more local analysis of the subject's use of the semiotic systems that Barthes considered in his early career. Critics also resent his attention to personal reactions, sensations, and physiological preoccupations. To many readers, these analyses appear useless because they do not have the obvious political repercussions of his early writing on fashion and culture, for example. Here, a focus on the politics of negation seems to eclipse the pleasurable, when they are in fact inseparable for Barthes. In this context, what is particularly relevant to this study is *The Pleasure of the Text, A Lover's Discourse: Fragments,* and *Camera Lucida*'s emphasis on a loss of self, which relates to the erotic experience and to the political potential of *jouissance.* Barthes's late work enables a clarification of the positive aesthetic of formally innovative texts that have so far been confined to a primarily negative rhetoric. The loss of self that Barthes theorizes allows us to understand the erotic fusion of text and reader, a fusion that allows a mutual constitution of reader and open text.

The authors of *Plus, AVA, DICTEE,* and *VAS* exploit the erotic and political qualities of this mutual constitution. In fact, Barthes's and Maso's visions of literature are particularly close, as both think that, in a metonymic way, texts imply the presence of a body. Just as the room, the listener, and the performer are part of the instrument when someone plays music, the reader, in communion with the text, enables the activation of the system that animates it. Barthes and Maso consider the relationship to the text as a sensual dialogue, emphasizing "notions of language as heat and light, motion and stillness, a vibrant living thing capable of containing great emotion. Also fluid, shifting, elusive, fugitive, and darkness keep taking back. Bodies which make fragile amorphous, beautiful shapes for a moment and then are gone" (Maso *Rain Taxi*). Maso's novel presents such a fluid and vibrant language in her depiction of the thoughts of Ava Klein, a comparative literature professor who is dying of a rare cancer. Her thoughts intermingle with references and direct citations from Samuel Beckett, Jorge Luis Borges, Hélène Cixous, and Anaïs Nin—to cite only a few—as well as film transcripts. The novel does not follow a logical and chronological pattern but relies on repetitions, insistence, and loops of information to build the story of Ava Klein (see figure 3):

And now she seems a shadow saying, Goldfinch

Holding a yellow bird in her mouth

Saying, Satin gown,

Not a person

Alabaster beauty.

FIGURE 3. Carole Maso. *AVA* p. 149 (c) 1993 Dalkey Archive Press.

The sentence is broken down into lines augmenting its possible meanings, allowing the reader, in Maso's words, to "read any given line and any series of lines and put in as much of [his or her] own story or memory or anything to it" (personal interview). Hence, an excess of signification, often incompatible with the coherence of the narrative, is the occasion for the reader's interpretive foreplay with "the patina of consonants, the voluptuousness of vowels, a whole carnal stereophony" (*Pleasure* 66). This conception of literature confirms Cixous's belief that in reading and writing we experience language as physical.

For Cixous, "The process of writing is to circulate, to caress, to paint all the phenomena before they are precipitated, assembled, crystallized in a word" (*Rootprint* 18). In "Coming to Writing," Cixous implies that writing requires an opening of senses, provoking hybrid visions and sensations, an experience that breaks down the binary models she refutes. She thinks of these "in-between" sensations and visions in terms of the "Third body":

> What flows from my hand onto the paper is what I see-hear, my eyes listen, my flesh scans. [. . .] I am childhood, my mother sings, her alto voice. More! Encore! a lovely tongue licks at my heart, my flesh takes in the German that I can't make out. [. . .] Lay, hymn, milk. *Lieb!* Love. [. . .] I am woman, I make love, love makes me, a *Third Body* (*Troisième Corps*) comes to us, a third sense of sight, and our other ears [. . .] but in order for the third body to be written, the exterior must enter and the interior must open out. (53–54)

In this passage, the two bodies are associated with Cixous's body and her mother's body since she refers to her mother's voice as guidance for rhythms and sounds. The two bodies also relate to the body of writing, the work as a corpus: "Letters love me. *Leise*. Soft and low, I sense that I am loved by writing." Here, she hints at the physical relationship between the writer and language. The Third Body would thus come between both. The two bodies can also be understood as two bodies during sexual intercourse, for she alludes to two bodies whose combination provokes the surge of a third body. Finally, Pamela Banting conceives of *écriture féminine* as an "interlangue somewhere between patriarchal discourse and an as-yet-unknown language," which leads us to interpret the Third Body in similar terms here (236). The Third Body is the interlangue, both intermediary language and connection tongue, between the writer and the text. Each of the possible interpretations of the Third Body implies an exchange that provokes change.

The possibility of change and exchange through the Third Body relies on its position between the interior and exterior: it avoids the thinking process that separates the body and its environment, and its lawless realm enables new possibilities in writing. Nevertheless, critics of Cixous's theory question it because of her emphasis on the relationship between body and text. These scholars blame Cixous for essentialism since they understand *écriture féminine* as a mode of writing that relies on the essence of a woman and that is a receptacle for biological determinism and pre-cultural femininity. In other words, critics interpret Cixous's invitation for women to use their bodies as determining those bodies as the direct source of female writing.[6] However, Cixous does not conceptualize the body as a better precedence for writing. Rather, she is "thinking of the body as a pictogram, [which] opens up ways of theorizing [. . .] bodies and texts" (Banting 240). Cixous's "Sorties" and "The Laugh of the Medusa" elaborate on the Cartesian oppressiveness, which distinguishes between the intelligible and the sensual, as she claims that feminine writing relies on a writing of women's bodies. Hence, as Morag Shiach argues, in Cixous's work, "it is impossible to sustain the complete dichotomy between mind and body which offers the illusion of intellectual control at the cost of erasing, censoring, and hystericizing the body" (70). Body and text do not precede one another, nor are they the source of one another. Only when relinquishing the dichotomy between mind and body, physicality and spirituality, and concreteness and abstractedness can we appreciate Cixous's undertaking. *Ecriture féminine* and the Third Body are analytical tools that elucidate the relationship between an eroticization of language and the positive political production that occurs in *Plus, AVA, DICTEE,* and *VAS.*

·It may seem peculiar, however, to deal with eroticism in novels such as *Plus, AVA, DICTEE,* and *VAS* since, at the level of content, their primary focus is not sexuality. Barthes's theories on photography clarify this seeming contradiction. Barthes distinguishes the pornographic picture from the erotic picture:

> Pornography ordinarily represents the sexual organs, making them into a
> motionless object [. . .]. The erotic photograph, on the contrary (and it is

---

6. For instance, in her account of Cixous, Toril Moi tackles *écriture féminine* as an inconclusive Derridian practice because it calls for a return to the "voice," the origin of writing for women. Mary Jacobus dismisses *écriture féminine* as an essentialist practice because it ignores the social-historical narratives which women embody. Teresa Ebert believes that Cixous reifies the notion of body and language. And Gayatri Spivak expresses dissatisfaction with Cixous's exploration of the revolutionary potential of language.

its very condition), does not make the sexual organs into a central object; it may very well not show them at all; it takes the spectator outside its frame, and it is there that I animate this photograph and that it animates me. (*Camera* 58–59)

Hence, it is "as if the image launched desire beyond what it permits to see" (*Camera* 59). For Barthes, then, a text that does not represent sexuality at the level of content might actually be more erotic precisely because of what it omits. Celia Daileader notes that, for Barthes, "eroticism, paradoxically, makes absence palpable, which is to say, it un-makes it, or rather unmasks it, in all its semiotic glory" (29). For her, "eroticism is an effect of this very engagement with or teasing of verbal boundaries, is perhaps achieved by way of the illusion that one has touched the edge of the intelligible, the describable, the discursive. Eroticism entails the illusion (if it is one) that it is possible to touch the body directly" (22). The "teasing of verbal boundary" alludes to something "missing" in language but felt by the reader. Thus, the absence of overt sexuality in *Plus, AVA, DICTEE,* and *VAS* might call for a more powerful erotic response.

This erotic response relies on the excesses of language that Kristeva, Lecercle, Cixous, and Barthes associate with blissful experiences. Yet, in *Plus, AVA, DICTEE,* and *VAS,* the material existence of the text—the visual form of the page of a book and the visual signs on it—also participates in the erotic excesses of writing. Johanna Drucker's work on typography clarifies the importance of the materiality in works such as the ones studied here:

> All books are visual. Even books which rely exclusively on type, or on unusual materials, or those which contain only blank sheets have a visual presence and character. All books are tactile and spatial as well—their physicality is fundamental to their meaning. Similarly, the elements of visual and physical materiality participate in a book's temporal effect— the weight of paper, covers, endpapers or inserts, fold-outs or enclosures all contribute to the experience of a book. However, it is clear that there are books which maximize their visual potential by taking advantage of images, color, photographic materials, sequencing, juxtaposition or narratives. (*The Century* 197)

Because *The Body of Writing* focuses on such books, Drucker's theories are particularly useful. In the following excerpt from one of her essays, which enacts its claim in the progressive enlargement of the typeface of the text,

Drucker calls our attention to the material of writing, which is traditionally neglected from interpretation. Usually, what language "means" is favored:

> A prophylactic attitude attempts to protect the imagination from direct encounters with the world as the tongue, the hand, the arm, the fist around the pen, the fingers on the keyboard all reach into the heavy flesh of matter and are rewarded by the response of sensory experience.

> This does not make meaning. It only makes a space in which meaning comes to have its face pressed against the glass, waiting to break through beyond the mirror of its own pale image. (*Figuring* 55)

Drucker's work reveals that what we cast aside as framework or context in regard to writing cannot be separated from what texts express. Her theory of materiality is particularly useful when approaching the works of Maso, Cha, and Tomasula because these writers experiment with typography so that their texts are as visual as they are verbal. In calling attention to the page, the textures of language, and in inserting visual texts into their prose, these authors, like Drucker, "RESIS[T] THE **VERBAL** EXPECTATIONS THE CLEAN MACHINE OF **READING** [. . .], DISRUPTED **BY THE INTERFERING** SUBSTANCE WHICH **DISTRACTS** THE EYE" (*Figuring* 142).[7] The "interfering substance" of these texts forces us to realize that the *look* of the page is not a surplus—an accessory to or an illustration of the message of the text. In fact, "There is a visuality of language which is not imagistic, but specific to the quality of written language itself. Not an inherency, but an actuality, tangible, perceptible, specific, and untranslatable, understood and grasped as effect" (*Figuring* 109). Therefore, the material of the book is in constant engagement with it. As Drucker's choice of words attests, the physicality of writing calls for a bodily response: in the aforementioned essay, the hand that crafts the text's visual existence provokes a sensory response, and in the above excerpts, the materiality of the text adds a physical layer to the expressive form, which necessitates a different engagement of our eyes in reading. Thus, the text becomes comparable to a body: "LIKE ANY OTHER ORGANISM, [IT] **REJOICES IN** THE PINBALL GAMES OF TOUCH AND **UNCERTAINTY** WHICH MULTIPLY **THE** POSSIBLE ACTIVITIES FOR ENGAGEMENT WITH AN AUDIENCE

---

7. Drucker inserts another narrative in a smaller typeface in-between these lines, which adds to the distractive effect the essay theorizes.

EXCHANGE OF SATISFYING **CONVERSATION** LAID OUT ON THE TABLE TO SEDUCE THE EYE" (144).

The "seduction of the eye" is better understood in relation to the concept of the "haptic" in Deleuze and Guattari's work. The "haptic" derives from their exploration of "smooth spaces"—spaces such as the sea, steppe, ice, and deserts that are constituted by continuous variation of free action and "have no background, plane, or contour" (*A Thousand* 496). In such spaces, we cannot use visual models for points of reference; we cannot map out the surface of water, for example, which relies on small and continuous changes. Instead, we are forced to focus on the particularities of such surfaces. The exploration of smooth places leads Deleuze and Guattari to develop two modes of visuality. The "haptic," which allows us to consider space as tactile, as if caressed by our eyes, is opposed to the "optical" mode of seeing, whose goal is to identify the configuration of space and decipher shapes and images. During optical visions, we can see objects as distinct and identifiable because we are able, from a distance, to explore the surface and what is on it. On the contrary, during haptic visions, a movement close to the surface allows us to focus on components' multiple combinations instead of on their assemblage. In other words, clear referents are not present in the haptic mode because we cannot use a prearranged deciphering of the surface. As Brian Massumi notes, the haptic, in "tak[ing] up a tactile function," enables vision to "regathe[r] itself, enveloping its own links to its sensory outside" (158). This implies that the haptic vision weakens the separation between the subject and the surface, as opposed to the optical mode, where the subject demarcates itself from what it is observing.

Haptic visuality allows us to see surfaces as if we were touching them, and, as Claudia Benthien explains, touch brings awareness to the surface in contact with the subject but also to the subject's body (200). This dual awareness occurs when the boundaries between the subject's formation and the surface dissolve in an erotic conjunction. In avant-garde films, Laura Marks notes, viewers go through such conjunction when using their eyes as touching organs, thus blurring the barrier between themselves and the medium. The eye's tactile function allows the viewer to leave his or her own position, to become part of the world, and then to dialectically return to a subject position *in* the world. For Marks, this shift in positions "is erotic. In sex, what is erotic is the ability to move between control and relinquishing, between being giver and receiver. It's the ability to have your sense of self, your self-control, taken away and restored—and to do the same for another person" (*Touch* xvi). As a film critic, Marks links this taking and releasing of control to an alternation between close and far visions. In images, close proximity to the medium blurs our vision so that we barely recognize what we are seeing and pay more attention to the substance of the material. I wish to transpose such explorations of the haptic mode to the reading realm, not only because *Plus, AVA, DICTEE,* and *VAS* mix visual and textual media but also because thinking of our eyes in terms of touching or caressing elucidates the opportunity of a loss of self *through* a physical connection to a medium. By forcing readers to focus on their physical qualities, these books invite us to come closer to their medium (the ink, the print, the page) so that we "zoom" in and out on the object in hand, as in "haptic *visuality,*" when the "eyes themselves function like organs of touch" (Marks *Skin* 183; *Touch* 2).

In the photograph of Yu Guan Soon on page 24 of *DICTEE,* for example, the overexposed picture appears almost as a silhouette of the female character: "the melded contrast of the texture of the extreme white and extreme black" insists on the imperfection of the photographic medium, which draws attention to the black and white flecks that make up the picture (Hadfield 128). The details of the picture compare to a movement from the global to the local, which resists systematic knowledge. As Georges Didi-Huberman reveals, when exploring Gaston Bachelard's thoughts on details in visual arts, such movements introduce

> a division of the subject of close-up knowledge. It's as if the describing subject, by dint of cutting something local out of something global, came to disassociate his very act of knowledge [. . . .] [I]t's as if the describing subject, in the very "tearing-to-pieces" movement that constitutes the operation of the detail, instead of proceeding to the serene reciprocity of a totalization, redirected despite himself and *onto himself* the first, violent act of disintegration. (233)

Because the subject comes so close to the medium, he or she cannot reach a total vision, which he or she usually uses to construct knowledge. The close-up gaze provokes an interference with our habitual conceptual frameworks. In *VAS,* the close-up on page [352] does not allow us to understand the global message the image conveys (see figure 4):[8] The novel focuses on Square, a writer considering getting a vasectomy in a world whose absurdity compares, at times, to A. E. Abbott's *Flatland.* Square's research on the operation leads him to uncover documents on the modification and tech-

---

8. Because some pages are missing their number in *VAS,* I will refer to these pages in brackets hereafter.

nologization of bodies. A collage of data, theories, and pictures is presented parallel to his story; the following image is one of them. When facing this page, our vision comes so close to the skin that it is difficult to know which part of the body is represented, where the hair is situated, and what the red marks that appear on the skin are. It is impossible to draw global conclusions from the local picture or to make it fit within a system of knowledge about the body.[9]

For Marks, such interactions with the artistic material induce change. Indeed, throughout the haptic experience, the subject is changing its nature: it loses itself, achieves a new stability, then changes again, alternating between being one with the object and being exterior to it. This alternation allows mutual formation of the subject and the text, which triggers new possibilities of knowledge production and invites the subject to conceive of alternative ways to interact with texts and the world. In other words, McElroy's, Maso's, Cha's, and Tomasula's works propose new modes of interaction with literature and society, and they enable readers to practice them during their reading techniques.

In that sense, Marks's theory is useful to my interpretation of such texts, not only because McElroy, Maso, Cha, and Tomasula research the materiality of visual and linguistic elements but also because "Haptic images do not invite identification with a figure so much as they encourage a *bodily relationship* between the viewer and the image" (3 *Touch*; italics mine). This "bodily relationship" with the medium will be central in my reading of literature. But, while Marks underlines the changes that a viewer undergoes during his or her haptic experience, she does not address the ways in which this experience changes the reader's relationship to the medium itself. Didi-Huberman's work on experiences of *pan* is useful here because it explicates the repercussion of such experiences for our conception of art media. Didi-Huberman explores "a work of bedazzlement, in some sense, at once self-evident, luminous, perceptible, and obscure, enigmatic, difficult to analyze, notably in semantic or iconic terms; for it is a work or an effect of painting as colored material, not as descriptive sign" (248). He calls *pan* "the part of painting that interrupts ostensibly, from place to place, like a crisis or a symptom, the continuity of the picture's representational

---

9. While haptic experiences, like the experience of the detail, avoid the totalization of the vision, they focus even more on the surface, the material of the art. In other words, unlike the detail, they do not just isolate a local vision: "In a haptic relationship our self rushes up to the surface to interact with another surface. When this happens there is a concomitant loss of depth—we become amoebalike, lacking a center, changing as the surface to which we cling changes. We cannot help but be changed in the process of interacting" (*Touch* xvi).

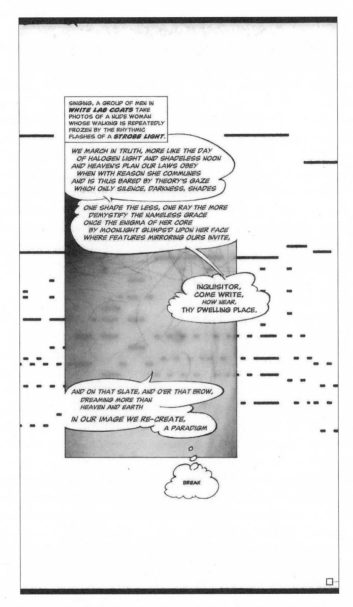

FIGURE 4. Steve Tomasula. *VAS: An Opera in Flatland* p. 352 (c) 2004 Steve Tomasula. The University of Chicago Press.

system"—the strange abstract figure of a stain by the lacemaker's hand in Jan Vermeer's *Lacemaker,* and the liquid projection that comes from the hat's fleece in Vermeer's *Girl with a Red Hat* (266).[10] Didi-Huberman uses Bergotte's description of Vermeer's painting to describe fragments that provoke "suspended" moments of visibility because of the intrusion of the painting material in our vision (259). Such intrusions occur in *VAS,* for example: page 257 bears the traces of brown and red liquids that appear vertically, disrupting the horizontal organization of the collage of web pages and writing (see figure 5). The stains disturb the deciphering of the image, as they partially hide some of the text and the "Replaceable you" web page. In that sense, they capture our attention and redirect it toward the color of the page, the ink on it, and the way it is organized, so that "such a zone [. . .] creates within the picture the equivalent of an explosion" (Didi-Huberman 252). Because the red and brown stains on the right hand side "propos[e], against the grain of representational function, a blaze of substance, color without fully controlled limit," they oppose the optical apparatus and allow us to focus on a haptic mode of perception instead (Didi-Huberman 252).

In drawing attention to its substance, the *pan* cannot be absorbed by the picture; it resists inclusion so that "once discovered, it remains problematic" (268). As Didi-Huberman indicates, the *pan* is close to the haptic because it supposes a collapse of spatial coordination, a "quasi-touching" of the image (270). But in addition to the haptic, it makes us "understand the fragile moment of a disfiguration that nonetheless teaches us what figuring is" (271). Because the novels studied in this project explore the limits of their medium by using pagination unconventionally, I wish to transpose the theory of the *pan* to the written realm. Didi-Huberman himself alludes to connections between the *pan* in paintings and semiotic disruption, but he does not elaborate on them. I will explore the *pan* effects in the texts studied here, especially in *AVA*'s use of white space, which, as we shall see, highlights the materiality of the page.

---

10. As Luke Gibbons notes, it is "difficult to locate an English word—*patch, facet, section, segment*—that encompasses the full range of meaning Didi-Huberman plays with in the term *pan*" (71) The word "*pan*" also refers to an "area," "expanse," "zone," and "stretch," and Didi-Huberman borrows the idea and the figure from Marcel Proust's description of Vermeer's *View of Delft:* "'That's how I ought to have written,' he [Bergotte] said. 'My last books are too dry, I ought to have gone over them with a few layers of colour, made my language precious in itself, like this little patch of yellow wall'" (*The Captive* 185). "C'est ainsi que j'aurais dû écrire. Mes derniers livres sont trop secs, il aurait fallu passer plusieurs couches de couleur, rendre la phrase en elle-même précieuse, comme *ce petit pan de mur jaune*" (*La prisonnière* 222; my emphasis).

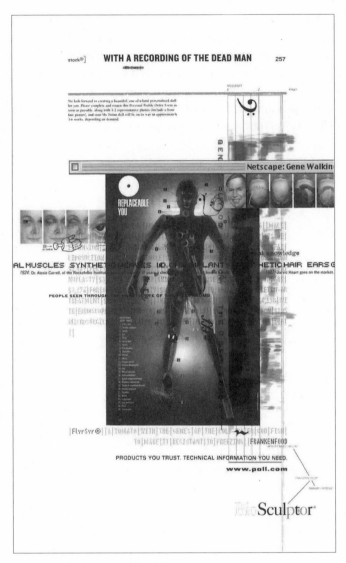

FIGURE 5. Steve Tomasula. *VAS: An Opera in Flatland* p. 257 (c) 2004 Steve Tomasula. The University of Chicago Press.

The consideration McElroy, Maso, Cha, and Tomasula give to textual materiality enables us to experience alternative relationships between reader and text. Their fictions call for a fusion between the cultural and physiological characteristics of reading: in engaging in a physical reading methodology, we concomitantly reconsider the cultural models that have excluded the body from intellectual activities such as reading. Thus, readings of formally innovative writing that have emphasized only cultural reconsiderations overlook the pleasurable sensuality inseparable from them. In the discussion of *Plus, AVA, DICTEE,* and *VAS* that follows, I explore this pleasurable production.

c h a p t e r   t w o

Semiotics and Erotics in
Joseph McElroy's *Plus*

> The brightness that was the Sun or from the Sun passed him many
> times between what he knew and what he nearly knew. Sleep was
> on one side, then on the other, never on both, also at times on nei-
> ther. The *word* for sleep was on only one side but now had come
> to be an audible line along the middle between the two sides.
>
> —Joseph McElroy, *Plus* (7)

The above excerpt from the first pages of *Plus* introduces some
of the key themes of the novel: knowledge, language, and bodily matters,
all of which feel in "between," "sid[ed]," in "the middle." This state of in-
between-ness is the result of a science experiment that has sent the disembodied brain of a scientific researcher into orbit between the earth and the
sun. The project, Operation Travel Light, has programmed the brain, Imp
Plus, to send information to Ground about his reactions to sunlight, which
it must do through the machine Cap Com. During the experiment, the Inter-
planetary Monitoring Platform on Earth is concerned with maintaining the
energy levels of Imp Plus. While the brain's interest in the "Sun" adheres
to the experiment's preparatory work and outcome, his abstract and poetic
considerations on sunlight, knowledge, and language foreshadow a displacement of the scientific into the erotic realm. The passage also sets up
Imp Plus's confused state and his center-less position: he attempts to situate himself with respect to the Sun, but his statements are tentative: "The
brightness that was the Sun or from the Sun" (7). Here, the "Sun" becomes

an entity, an actor, with Imp Plus in the sky, but the brightness automatically associated with sunlight is in question. *Plus* keeps disrupting these kinds of automatisms and the ways in which we use language to conceive of them. The structure of the phrase "The brightness that was the Sun" resembles a definition, and the qualification "or from the Sun" adds more specificity to the statement, as if the narrative is striving to be as exact as possible. Surprisingly, even though the sentence feels like a definition, its meaning remains unclear. Similarly, the difference between "what he knew and what he nearly knew" appears to be a clarification, but it is impossible to locate what or where "between" is. Such gaps between how sentences feel and what they mean express the confused state of the narrator. In looking for an accurate mode of expression, Imp Plus makes unclear statements: How can brightness actually pass "between what he knew and what he nearly knew"? What is the "one side"? And "the other"? How can "the word for sleep" be "on one side" but also "in the middle between two sides"? Here, is Imp Plus referring to the right and left parts of the brain? Is he describing sides of his brain that might have been cut or wired? Is he talking about the sides of the orbit that may encounter the sun in rotation? Perhaps these sides are not physical but metaphorical poles that shape his expressions. In fact, if we take Imp Plus's statement literally, the "Sun" generates the layers of knowledge that he wrestles with, which opens the novel to the poetic reinvention of the narrator. This reinvention, like *délire,* is influenced by "flows of energy" and the "emergence of sense out of nonsense" (Lecercle 198). In the above example, McElroy's play on sounds and patterns—the repetition of the sound [s] and the rhythmic accumulation of clauses in the second sentence—calls attention to the materiality of the language in question.

McElroy's interest in linguistic materiality is often paired, as it is in *Plus,* with scientific and epistemological explorations. His fictions involve a variety of disciplines (chaos theory, cybernetics, biology, data processing, geology, botany, genetics, ecology, relativity, as well as others) to question the relationship between science and language. McElroy has produced eight novels reflecting on these disciplines and the ways that human experience, seen as a collaborative network, can be conveyed within the constraints of the linear process of writing. His novels are intricately composed, dwelling on the linguistic nature of narrative, and involve experimentation in narration, syntax, and structure. *A Smuggler's Bible* (1966) presents a reflection on sacred texts and offers an opportunity for the unusual assemblage of eight stories that David, the narrator, reads aboard a transatlantic ship. *Hind's Kidnap: a Pastoral on Familiar Airs* (1969) is an inquiry into kidnappings, the deciphering of which relies on a "dense nightmare anonymity—New York, Brooklyn Heights, terrible genealogy, the self in relation to others" ("Joseph McElroy"). *Ancient History: A Paraphase* (1971) is composed of detective puzzles that question the meanings and causes of psychological evolution, as field theories are applied to people's lives and contaminate the processes of perception, thinking, and writing. *Lookout Cartridge* (1974) focuses on the life of a man named Cartwright after he makes a movie that by chance has recorded terrorist activities. The film disappears and Cartwright puts his life in danger to find it and understand its disappearance. *Women and Men* (1987) is an evocation of the connections between communication systems. In the 1,192-page novel, McElroy ambitiously creates communicative and integrative systems that make up the structures of our lives. *The Letter Left to Me* (1998) presents a boy reading a letter from his dead father, the written words of which enable a mental discussion between the two characters. *Actress in the House* (2003) tells the story of actress Becca and lawyer Daley, as they "begin a precarious period of discovery, [. . .] slipping a boundary to both past and future" ("Joseph McElroy"). These different examples show McElroy playing with intimate life, technological data, and scientific systems as themes and structures, allowing "a certain conjunction [. . .] of ordinary women and men, children, family, domesticity—that whole area—and this other, we may say *larger,* matter, which involves technology and science and disaster, urban planning and that whole thing" ("Some Bridge" 12). For McElroy, science is not an abstraction isolated from human life; rather it is part of people's intimate and personal experience. Despite this, his use of science has often been interpreted as making his novels cold, less interested in human beings than in the complexity of globalizing systems.

Most critics approaching McElroy pay considerable attention to his use of technology and science, identifying links between his work and complex systems. Steffen Hantke and John Kuehl consider McElroy's novels as demonstrations of conspiracy and paranoia because of the political debates inherent in his fictions and because of their systematic narrative structures. Tom Leclair uses systems theory to approach McElroy's use of form, language, and literary construction. Tony Tanner and Frederick Karl focus on the treatment of space and field that invites readers to approach the texts as maps. While these readings have underlined important traits in McElroy's work, they fail to realize that the author questions de-humanized representations of science and technology. In fact, for McElroy, "science reaches out of the lab into everyday work and survival and community," so that in a novel like *Plus,* the use of scientific concepts and technical terminology attempts to express accurately the complexity of the world, not to alienate humanity

("Plus *Light*"). In pointing out the limits of traditional models that divorce abstractedness from the tangible particulars of life, McElroy invites us to rethink such models, their foundations, and their repercussions in our lives. What is more, when critics separate the abstract and intimate explorations of McElroy's work, they also overlook its sensual enjoyment. In other words, seeing McElroy's novels as systematic renderings of human lives clarifies his debunking of societal organizations, but McElroy's work does not limit itself to a political debunking: it also generates a sensual fusion between reader and text, which clarifies its positive potential. Consequently, rather than separating science, technology, intimacy, and sensuality in McElroy's fictions, I would like to embrace them in my analysis of *Plus*. This approach has been put forth by Joseph Tabbi in his study of McElroy's novels in relation to "Midcourse Corrections," a personal essay fragmented by interviews conducted by the author. Unlike Tabbi, however, I stay away from the biographical lens to analyze *Plus,* as this lens implies that the novels themselves do not challenge the dichotomy between science and intimate life.

In the novel, the bodiless brain starts growing a new kind of body, one built by his past emotions. Imp Plus's explorations of his new "body" are rooted in the flashes of past sensations and desires that come back to him. As Imp Plus recollects his fragmented life, he re-experiences it through intense sensory moments: "He had been thinking what would come and remembering what he was to become in four weeks. This thinking had been clear and it had been touched by desire; so it came to him now in orbit. [. . .] [T]his was new, this was not remembering" (63). The re-experience of desire progressively penetrates the machine-like thinking process the scientists have set up for Imp Plus. When desire merges with Imp Plus's thoughts, his senses become the driver of his communication. Therefore, this desire becomes not only a memory but also Imp Plus's motive during the experiment.

Imp Plus's articulation of his past and present desires surfaces unusually since, in planning for the experiment, Imp Plus had focused on the technical data necessary to his survival in space. He explains that he has "prepared not to remember but remembered just the same though not the word for it" (174). Although he had prepared to remember some words useful for the experiment, he cannot now focus on the *meaning* of these words alone, as the opening of this chapter has exemplified. Not remembering the vocabulary needed to communicate his raw emotions requires that he fall back on the technological words he has memorized for the purposes of the experiment. Consequently, the scientific experiment (its technical data and vocabulary) enables Imp Plus to counteract the efficiency of the technical terminology, transforming it into an idiosyncratic and intimate language.

Here, it becomes clear that Imp Plus, in keeping with the traditional scientific models of the NASA experiment, attempts to divide technological systems and intimate life. His failure in separating the two reveals that they are much more interrelated than dominant paradigms assert.

In *Plus*, the use of scientific vocabulary and archetypes works as surplus phenomena that disrupt traditional structuring and reading. Therefore, the technicality of this language adds an excess of signification which is incompatible with the coherence of the narrative at times. For instance, the repetition of terms such as "chlorella" or "chloroplasts" is unusual in literature, which may be why readers emphasize the complex and cold attributes of McElroy's writing. However, the technical terminology is not meant to complicate the reading of the text or to alienate the reader. Words like "chlorella" and "chloroplasts," for example, become part of a poetic use of language: "the chlorella and the chloroplasts that he found himself comprehending—or seeing—and came from the unwrapping map of the Sun" (34). The reader may or may not know that "chlorella" refers to "a unicellular green alga," and that a "chloroplast" is a plastid containing chlorophyll, but Imp Plus's unusual use of language (what does it mean to comprehend the chlorella and the chloroplasts? What exactly is the unwrapping map of the sun?) allows the reader to penetrate Imp Plus's experience of the world, one that does not rely on a traditional use of language. As I hope to show, the opacity of scientific words that have only a vague association for the reader forces him or her to focus on the materiality of language rather than on the words themselves, allowing an erotic relationship to language.

Christine Brooke-Rose analyzes the materiality of language in the novel to show that the technicality of scientific vocabulary renders McElroy's prose poetic. She notes that "McElroy [. . .] is interested in the sentence less for its abstract structure than for its contractions, its ambiguities, its qualities of density and clarity, of obstacle and absence of obstacle, or, in more conventional terms, its aesthetic quality" (288). This disrupts a traditional access to signification: the meaning of a word fluctuates. As a result, Brooke-Rose contends, Imp Plus's use of words relies on nonreferential language, "word-play and repetition, inversion, paradox, or language to point to and go beyond language," which introduces poetry into fiction writing (287). Building on Brooke-Rose's demonstration, I explore such language in the context of Imp Plus's sexually charged memories and desire-filled experiences. These memories and experiences shape the narrator's unconventional mode of expression: for him, language becomes an embodied and erotic medium of communication and reconstruction that escapes the needs and goals of the scientific framework.

My insistence on the erotic qualities of language is in line with Donna Haraway's theory of the cyborg.[1] In her model, the cyborg is a new entity that welcomes the human and the machine without making one superior to the other. It is also free of a binary logic. For Haraway, the "cyborg myth is about transgressed boundaries, potent fusions, and dangerous possibilities which progressive people might explore as one part of needed political work" (154). Haraway provides "an argument for pleasure in the confusion of boundaries," and adds that "From the point of view of pleasure in [. . .] potent and taboo fusions, made inevitable by the social relations of science and technology, there might indeed be a feminist science" (150, 173). Science fiction provides a "catalogue of promising and dangerous monsters who help redefine the pleasures and politics of embodiment and feminist writing" (179). However, an analysis of *how* these fictions "redefine the pleasures and politics of embodiment and feminist writing" is missing from her essay. For Haraway, "Only by being out of place could we take intense pleasure in machines," which implies that the breaking down of boundaries itself provides pleasure (180). Thanks to Kristeva's work, I wish to elaborate on how pleasure can come out of the conflating of these boundaries.[2]

Kristeva, read conjointly with *Plus,* is valuable for this analysis because she clarifies the ways in which the blurring of science and human experience, and that of physical and nonphysical properties, creates pleasure. On the one hand, Kristeva provides an analysis of the linguistic system that places the libidinal nonexpressive qualities of texts at the center of language's structure, and so offers a vocabulary for naming the poles of power that frame Imp Plus's evolution. On the other hand, what is particularly interesting about *Plus* is the integration of the Semiotic on a linguistic level (through the sonic and rhythmic qualities of the text), and its allegorical function within the plot (through the representation of poles of power comparable to the Semiotic and the Symbolic). Thus, *Plus* allows us to reflect on and practice embodied paradigms of knowledge. Kristeva hints at the importance of the

---

1. For a detailed discussion of Haraway's work in relation to *Plus,* see Salvatore Proietti's "Joseph McElroy's Cyborg *Plus.*"

2. David Porush underlines pleasure as a mode of resistance to scientific discourse that views humans as machines. He notes that, in *Plus,* passages that combine "the false technical language created by Imp Plus to name his new experience [. . .] have a haunting pleasant effect" (195). While Porush briefly mentions the pleasurable qualities of language here, he analyzes in detail the "de-automatization of language" (178). Using Viktor Shklovsky's theory, he claims that Imp Plus's unusual use of language forces the reader to look at words in an unfamiliar way. However, Porush does not elaborate on the relationship between pleasure and de-automatization by asking, for example, how language leads to pleasure, and how this pleasure provides a resistance to scientific discourses. I attempt to clarify these matters in this chapter.

body in relation to knowledge because libidinal traces pierce language, but her claim for revolutionary changes concentrates mostly on the power of the Semiotic, not on the embodied access to knowledge it enables. In contrast, *Plus* goes further in its presentation of a body that grows out of fragments of language, reminding us that language and the body are not isolated and that political changes occur not only through ideological reconsiderations but also through embodied practices. Therefore, *Plus* helps us understand how an erotics of language directs us toward a practice and reevaluation of the body's role in interpretation, which emphasizes the positive outcomes in Kristeva's theory.

Kristeva's concept of the Symbolic, which relies on the rules of logical discourse whose goal is limited to communication, is akin to Cap Com's logical directions to Imp Plus: "GLUCOSE IN ERROR. IMP PLUS ARE YOU GETTING STRESS?" (56). Cap Com appears in the novel as the Symbolic since its voice is the voice of a computer or a machine placed on Earth. It also brings to mind the voice of pilots in airplanes, which elicits a parallel to Imp Plus's situation. The interruptions of Cap Com constantly challenge the development of Imp Plus's semiotic experience: "CAP COM TO IMP PLUS AGAIN IMP PLUS SAY AGAIN WATER WHAT WATER?"; "CAP COM TO IMP PLUS: CHECK FREQUENCY CHECK FREQUENCY" (14); "CAP COM DO YOU READ ME?" (19). CAP COM repeats "CAP COM TO IMP PLUS" to establish contact since Cap Com and Imp Plus cannot see one another, but paradoxically, this establishment of contact introduces a formal rupture in communication that destroys the possibility of a human-like interaction. In addition, this technological speech is abbreviated, and it leaves out articles. It is a telegraphic mode of communication that uses only imperatives and concentrates on the practical effect of language: Cap Com focuses strictly on the message. The machine needs clear and definite information about Imp Plus's physical state.

The switch between upper and lower case is significant: in calling attention to the typefaces of the novel, McElroy reminds us of the power dynamics that are associated with typography. As Drucker notes:

> the design of typefaces is the result of a certain tension between technological constraints and the conceptual imagining of how a letter should look to function as an effective element of communication. The legacy of handwriting, touch, and gesture that shaped metal type in early decades of 15th-century Italian humanist faces was as much a result of an ideology as a necessary outcome of material constraints. ("Typographic Intelligence" 9)

The change of typefaces in *Plus* serves the shifts of power in the narrative, but it also attests to the relationship between language and technology, which is central to Imp Plus's story. Because the novel invites us to reconsider how we use language, it comes as no surprise that the typography used to convey messages is also in question. As Margaret Re notes, "No matter how uncomprehending the reader may be of the type that is used as a tool to knit together thoughts and ideas, the reader's understanding of the text *is* shaped by the typography and the way it is structured" ("Reading" 29). *Plus*'s use of upper and lower case supports the narrative's exploration of a rediscovery of language that, for the reader, also includes a re-acquaintance with the typefaces of books; we take them for granted as much as the language Imp Plus refigures.

The syntax and content of the passages in upper case evolves as the book goes on. At the beginning, Imp Plus communicates in technical terms similar to Cap Com's: "Imp Plus transmitted the velocity for his synchronous orbit: IMP PLUS VELOCITY 1.9" (14). Imp Plus's sentences focus on the symbolic aspects of language, enhancing the information the machine needs. Cap Com also frames Imp Plus's dialogue within symbolic constraints: "THIS MORNING WHAT. IMP PLUS. YOU SAID THIS MORNING. THIS MORNING WHAT? COME IN IMP PLUS" (75). Cap Com reminds Imp Plus of the symbolic rules requiring him to make sense, to deliver a message. Imp Plus explains, "Ground would not let him think as he would about this beautiful gyro-norm he had made himself amid the former jolting spins" (175–176). Cap Com, attached to "Ground," does not allow Imp Plus to express his semiotic experience. Only the result of the experiment matters. But Imp Plus progressively distances himself from the influence of Cap Com, decides that he is not just a "semi-conductor," and rejects the symbolic paradigm (168):

> And he was more touched and still more touched on this blind spot and something called laughter passed through him into his head bent toward the space between points and coil, and this laughter wasn't like that other laughter that grayed the graph in the green room. For this laughter, he now saw, was radiant. (20)

Imp Plus states that "he was more touched," which implies that when he was "alive," he was not as much in touch with his sensations. It is also important that Imp Plus relates the "other laughter," that which he remembers from the past, to "the graph in the green room." In his association of past laughter with the green room, whence he was put into orbit, he clearly links this less "radiant" laughter to his experiences of the lab. As he detaches himself from the Symbolic, he experiences more "radiant" sensations. Because of this progressive rejection of the symbolic power, his interactions with Cap Com have changed:

> IMP PLUS TO GROUND, IMP PLUS TO GROUND. WHAT HAPPENS TO BRAIN'S THREE-DIMENSIONAL MAP OF RETINA WHEN NO RETINA IS LEFT TO PLUG INTO? WHAT HAPPENS TO FLAMING GLAND BELOW DISCOLORED OPTIC CROSSING WHEN BRAIN DISPERSES? HAVE SEEN AND BEEN BUT DO NOT KNOW. (208)

At this point of the narrative, we realize that Imp Plus is no longer focusing on the physical or biochemical state of his brain. He is not trying to be consistent and neutral as the experiment would like him to be; his inconsistencies and his ability to change the scientific logic are characteristics of the Semiotic. In emphasizing growth, *Plus* reveals that through change, Imp Plus, literally a *sujet en procès,* can resist the stability of the Symbolic. I emphasize the concept of growth, as it is crucial to changes the Semiotic provokes, and it clarifies in Kristeva's paradigm the political consequences of pleasure Haraway identifies in her cyborg model. In other words, Imp Plus's growth reveals that the novel's political outcome relies not only on what it responds to or disrupts but also on what grows out of it. In fact, McElroy

> wanted to give a feeling of rudiments that would parallel the subtraction of the body that the main character began with before we knew him. But the story is growth, and about beginning with something shrunk—narrowly cut, reduced, fundamental, in this case the brain and what soon becomes evident, a field of character—and the movement then is to expand by painful inches. (personal interview)

During this painful expansion, Imp Plus, whose name also plays on the word "impulse," relies on semiotic drives to confront the symbolic rationale of the experiment, thereby allowing language to be a site of pleasure, not only of transmission of information.

In Kristeva's model, this eroticization of language takes place when the Semiotic reconnects with the pre-*thetic,* the nonlinguistic mode that relies on libidinal drives. Imp Plus stresses his center-less pre-*thetic* situation:

> He gathered himself to see the algae beds and other plant tests he now saw he had lived with but not thought of. And he gathered himself to see now

the radius-spindles of his own changing Sun flow down the tube from that underhouse near what had been the bun or little brain. He gathered himself as suddenly to see sight membranes that had gone from the limbs into the cerebrum and grown or ranged to the top [. . .]. Gathered himself to see among the limb bodies now armed with substance parts of the brain lean toward focus.

And he gathered, or came to feel, that the gathering of different distances into focus was like the muscle pricks of spasm-flows of charge. (124)

The repetition of "he gathered himself" works as a musical refrain in the passage and alludes to a non-*thetic* conceptualization of himself as continuous with the surrounding plants. The recurrence of sounds also alludes to the difficulty Imp Plus has in gathering himself. The repetition "he gathered" is subjected to variation in the second paragraph: "the gathering." His focus is not on "himself" anymore, which evokes a change in his perception of his own identity. He acquires a fragmented, non-unified body.

Moreover, we read: "Imp Plus remembered words that he did not know. [. . .] Imp Plus had been in another shape, its word now gone. Imp Plus knew the word *word* and the word *idea,* but not what one was" (4). In relearning "who he is," or how language would define him, he raises questions about his identity. Imp Plus's new state also allows him to redefine himself. Here, "literary practice is seen as exploration and discovery of the possibilities of language; as an activity that liberates the subject from a number of linguistic, psychic, and social networks; as a dynamism that breaks up the inertia of language" (Kristeva qtd. in Roudiez 2). This experimental or exploratory relation to his own words can be seen in passages where the materiality of speech and comprehension strike him as new and puzzling:

Him.
    He found it on his mouth and in his breath. *Him.* A thing in all of him. But now he wasn't sure. He saw he'd felt this *him* in the brain. But where was it now? In too many centers. (114)

Imp Plus's lack of body and his position in space renders his identity hybrid. He sees his identity as un-centered, very much like a pre-oedipal subject whose "fragmented body" is "divided into erogenous zones" (*Revolution* 22). However, his past life, organized by the Symbolic, makes him wonder about his status. When stating "A semi-conductor. This was what Imp Plus was," Imp Plus categorizes his identity in a symbolic way (104). The shift in Imp Plus's perspective on his identity materializes the semiotic and symbolic influences on his development. To use Kristeva's words, Imp Plus's experiment "exposes the subject to impossible dangers relinquishing his identity in rhythm, dissolving the buffer of reality in a mobile discontinuity" (*Revolution* 169). Imp Plus's experience reveals the difficulty of positioning oneself within an environment, as well as the power of the semiotic disruptions that challenge linguistic structures and the *thetic* mode. As the novel progresses, the semiotic activity grows and modifies the character's conceptualization of his selfhood.

Imp Plus's considerations about his selfhood lead him to understand himself in terms that resist Ground's definition of his status. By resisting the Symbolic in this way, Imp Plus becomes more human: he is not just a machine, giving inputs on bodily fluid levels; he also has a personality. His semiotic resistance to the Symbolic associates with self-definition, which we can trace in his use of language and in the depiction of his environment: his semiotic representations become metaphors for people, places, and emotions instead of descriptions of them. Since the emergence of the Semiotic re-connects with the erotic drives of the pre-*thetic,* it is not surprising to see Imp Plus's negation of the *thetic* through his recollection of sexual encounters. Imp Plus interrelates the scientific requirements of the experiment (borrowing vocabulary from it) and memories of sexual experiences: "He had looked into an ingrown body of mouth upon grooves and arches of a tongue laid with velvet nipples of light-receptor cells" (153). His recollections unify the specific words of the experiment ("ingrown," "grooves," "light-receptor cells") and erogenous body parts ("mouth," "tongue," "nipples"). Sexual and scientific emotions become mixed in Imp Plus's mind, as each scientific word relates to an erotic zone. The effect is a blurring of differences and the creation of new entities: the "mouth" has a body; "light-receptor cells" have "velvet nipples." Science and Eros bleed into one another, and language spreads the erotic sensations of Imp Plus. The blurring of the scientific and the erotic accompanies the blurring of all separate identities: "how to mouth the difference, for was there a difference between a *her* mouth and a *him* mouth?" (154). Imp Plus alludes to the arbitrariness of signifying processes but also to the merging of bodies during sexual activities. His non-*thetic* position enables him to merge his body, or what is left of it, with scientific tools.

We realize this when paying attention to the fluid relationship between words, Imp Plus and his environment, and his past and present. Imp Plus's "logic," like *délire,* avoids the fixity of the symbolic experiment. This vision circumvents the straightforwardness and regimentation of the symbolic reports he is supposed to make:

> Distances dividing down faint dual troughs of belly that were not those
> lighted bellies of the brain now stretched like limbs seeking to become their
> source. Bellies curving in along beside suddenly much more hair which also
> was not fingers but then became fingers with blood red that loved him,
> someone else's fingers. (128)

The brain's sensual remembrance eroticizes the scientific lab. The repetitions of "fingers" and "belly" and the recurrence of plosive sounds ([d], [t], [b], and [g]) participate in this eroticization. The text acquires musicality through the repetition of these sounds. Imp Plus connects two body parts with the word "of." This gives the image of a strange body with "lighted bellies of the brain." We also note the changeable characteristics of the "fingers," as the hair "which also was not fingers but then became fingers with blood red that loved him." The correlation of the fingers with the hairy parts of the bellies denotes sexual activity, but the "blood red" brings us back to the operating table. The phrase "that loved him" turns back to the sexual activities. The coming and going between different poles on a thematic level—lovemaking and operation, sexuality and physiology—blur the boundaries between the scientific and the sexual, calling the reader's attention to words' movements in the text.

Hence, *Plus* puts the power of the Semiotic into practice, confirming that the Semiotic, through its constant changes, disrupts the *thetic,* or as Lecercle puts it, "the actions and passions of our body" taint language so that it "loses its capacity to communicate" (7). In *Plus,* this occurs through disruptions of meaning and grammatical structures. Imp Plus's mis-constructed sentences challenge grammatical rules, beginning chapters with a phrase such as "which meant" and using words ambiguously without definite reference (154). His linguistic evolution enables the re-emergence of the semiotic *chora,* as "rhythmic, lexical, even syntactic changes disturb the transparency of the signifying chain and open it up to the material crucible of its production" (*Revolution* 101). Indeed, Imp Plus's sentences usually avoid a correct grammatical path:

> The word came in a voice once his though not now just pulses on a fre-
> quency reaching further and further back to Earth, for that was Ground
> where his body was except a piece which he must call *brain* but was a piece
> of body blown off up the tube and axis and distance of distance where the
> curves of his chest would not return to him nor his chest hairs like fingers,
> fingers in the Sun if he could only stop but he could not. (128)

This sentence amasses clauses introduced by "and," "but," "where," "which," and "for." However, commas are sometimes missing, so that it is difficult to differentiate when "and" is adding information (such as "and distance of distance") and when it links two terms (such as "and further"). In addition, the use of "but" is inconsistent. We expect the conjunction to express opposition: it sometimes does ("but he could not") and sometimes does not ("call *brain* but was a piece of body blown off up the tube"). In the latter case, the brain is a "piece of body blown off the tube," so "but" is misleading. The grammatical structure of this passage negates the symbolic emphasis on the communication of a message and challenges the reader's understanding of Imp Plus's situation.

Imp Plus's experimentations with the texture of the words and with the way they sound and combine with one another directly address the resurfacing of the Semiotic. It becomes clear when he invents words:

> Looking, he did not know what to say of the whole thing he saw he was, whose seeing he also was.
>
> Where once there has been four wendings or faldoreams or shearows or morphogens, division had made many, and many one. (142)

As he makes up words, Imp Plus plays with language and enjoys the unmotivated experience of a combination of sounds. *Plus* relies on the meaning of words, but it also invites the reader to pay close attention to "the part of language that cannot be accounted for, that part that doesn't mean: nonsense, tones, rhythms" (Oliver 92). The protagonist's activity clearly correlates with the libidinal pleasure delineated in the works of Kristeva and Lecercle. In McElroy's work, these libidinal impulses alter the rhythms of the text, inviting a physical relationship to language, which the novel emphasizes through the shifts from "[h]e *found* it all around" (the first sentence of the novel) to "Imp Plus *felt* it all around" (3, 184; my emphasis). This stress on feeling in relation to language underlines rhythms and sounds, as they constitute a layer of signification that transgresses the order of the Symbolic and releases *jouissance*. Rhythms and flows relate to the reading of *Plus* since Imp Plus's experiment forces him to pay particular attention to his biological reactions while this scientific attention also activates the libidinal process at the root of the Semiotic.

Such physical awareness reappears in a life that Imp Plus wanted to limit to scientific data, which prevents him from translating fluxes of bodily impressions into language. The necessity for Imp Plus to focus on his physiological life allows him to express the "pulses going to Earth from Imp Plus" (3). As the scientific experiment forces him to check the levels and frequencies of his bodily fluids, he is paradoxically invited to explore his bodily rhythms, a semiotic activity that challenges the logic of the experiment, as his pulses become expressive: they are not limited to measurable materials. Imp Plus underlines, for instance, that "through the message pulses Imp Plus knew a thing more than what they told. The message pulses came through this change" (89). Here, science and Eros interconnect because the scientific means of action interacts with the libidinal pulses: repetitions and rhythms, in accordance with his body fluxes, shape his enunciations. Akin to *délire*, these nonexpressive patterns penetrate the text in its rhythms and incoherent grammatical structures, inviting a physical relationship between the reader and language.

Such rhythms and structure emerge from the novel's opening, describing the first minutes of the brain's realization of its state, through the devices of symmetry and asymmetry, and of repetition and creation:

> He found it all around. It opened and was close. He felt it was himself, but felt it was more.
>
> It nipped open from outside in and from inside out. Imp Plus found it all around. He was Imp Plus, and this was not the start.
>
> Imp Plus caved out. There was a lifting all around, and Imp Plus knew there was no skull. This lifting was good. But there had been another lifting and he had wanted it, but then that lifting had not been good. He did not want to get back to it. He did not know if that lifting had been bad. But this new lifting was good. (3)

The first two sentences are each composed of five words: subject-verb-complements. However, the syntax of the second sentence slightly changes because "and" introduces a second verb. The rhythm of the sentence is still close to that of the first, yet the balance introduced by "and" makes the second sentence sound different, and it makes it more complex. The simplicity of the sentences connects them, but there is a small evolution in the rhythm through the changes of the syntax. The first two verbs are in the active voice. The third one, which is connected to "opened" by "and," is not in the passive voice; however, we almost read it as passive since "opened" is associated with "closed" in our mind. This is an example of the way the text plays with the construction of an order to disorient or deconstruct it. This disruption enables the experience of the Semiotic for the reader because it draws attention to the rhythms and variations of the text and away from their informational content.

The following sentence lets us come back to a symmetrical movement with the repetition of "he felt it was," enabling the text to shift from irregularity to regularity and thereby constructing a leitmotif. We also see that a movement toward both the inside and the outside takes place in the beginning of the novel, if we pay attention to the sentence "It nipped open from outside in and from inside out." The sentence branches into an excess of repetition through contamination of the repeated phrases. The repetition of "opened," "close," "open," "outside," "inside," and "out" enables an inhalation and exhalation movement. Imp Plus, out of the earth, communicates with Ground. His brain, his mind, usually connected to inner characteristics, is cut off from his body, the outer part of his person. In other words, though we usually conceive of the brain as inside our body, Imp Plus's experience complicates this opposition. In *Plus,* the creation of a new locus for thoughts and Imp Plus's position in the sky force the narration to center on communications and movements between inside and outside spaces.

McElroy's presentation of the inside and outside in a science fiction forecasts the research of digital texts where the inside and outside, in relation to the machine and the reader, are also central. This inside/outside dynamic is particularly striking in a novel like Jackson's *Patchwork Girl,* where the reader penetrates the multilayered narrative/body/monster/software. As Hayles indicates, reading Jackson's novel requires a "fluid movement between bodies inside texts and texts inside bodies[;] 'inside' is constantly becoming 'outside' becoming 'inside,' as if performing at the visible level of the text the linkages between different coding levels within the computer" (*My Mother* 160). Of course, in *Plus,* the inside and outside poles are not visual or computerized realities, but the science fiction premise of the book enables a bodily practice that foreshadows electronic literature's research in interactive embodied reading methods.

In McElroy's work, the inside and outside theme shapes the entire narrative: "the Sun wished to open constantly some wondrous inequity between inside cell and outside in the sea about it" (88). Imp Plus remembers that "Ground was outside the capsule, but it made sounds Imp Plus received inside. [. . .] The oblong cells on the panels caught Ground and got Ground from outside inside" (104). I identify the inside/outside movement with inhalation and exhalation patterns, a parallel theme in the novel. Here, I build on William Wilson's examination of the "image of movement—in and out," in which Wilson claims that McElroy's prose proposes "an elaboration of the rhythms of organs like the lungs, which imply affable fields of breathable air. The opposites or alternatives to the movements in a pulsating field are anything that is inert or incompatible. [. . .] McElroy's field, at its most intense and magnanimous, is a field of incompatibilities." Wilson's qualification of the breathed fields in McElroy's fiction emphasizes the role of the body and the acceptance of incompatibilities in language, which in Kristeva's model would be semiotic and in Lecercle's paradigm would be *délire*. Hence, while Wilson stresses the field qualities of breath, I am more interested in the embodiment of breath through language, as it accounts for the presence of linguistic pleasure in *Plus*.

The first paragraph of the book creates a system of coming in and going out—inhalation- and exhalation-like movements—that balances the text. In focusing on such breathing movements, one comes closer to Imp Plus's semiotic activity. In other words, the breathing rhythms of the narration— the medium of the story—reflect Imp Plus's evolution and his interaction with the Semiotic and the Symbolic.[3] The trope of breath, which inserts the physicality of language back into the text, appears not only in the rhythms but also in the content of the novel: "It made him a new nerve past breathing"; "The pain itself stretched, and this was a decay like breath breathed in but never out"; "Dragged also then by a memory grown new in the rungs by a reach of act's breath taken, inhaled, used, and given back by desire for act to then inhale"; "The shapes of breathings round and round changed but continued, continued to change"; and so forth (47, 53, 86–87, 144). Through these patterns and allusions to breath, McElroy calls our attention to the biological impulses that take part in communication. He explains:

> I think of breathing as not only being necessary for life but as associated with intake and outflow, with expansion and contraction, which is my work, my long sentences which like long passages then contract; long book, shorter book.
>
> When I am feeling more confident with everything, I like to think that this breathing that we do, which keeps the oxygen coming in and is associ-

---

3. The trope of breath is omnipresent in McElroy's work, in particular in *Women and Men,* where breath even affects the organization of the novel, expanding the possibility of the narrative structure since sub-sections called "breathers" allow a change of point of view in the narration. The "breathers" stand in-between chapters: "BETWEEN US: A BREATHER AT THE BEGINNING," for example. These "breathers" offer "meditative spaces where the reader can rest—or, in McElroy's language, take a deep 'breath'—and contemplate the mysterious connections between events and characters" (Gleason). In *Plus,* the trope is not used to structure the chapters, but it influences the rhythms of the sentences, offering a formal rendition of the struggles between the symbolic and semiotic poles.

ated with speaking, making sounds, connects us with everything, or at least with everything alive. (personal interview)

Plus focuses on the breathing rhythm that penetrates both the semantic doublings and the structure of sentences. McElroy's interest in the breathing abilities of a sentence brings him close to Charles Olson and Allen Ginsberg, for whom the page and poetic line are functions of the human breath. In "Projective Verse," Olson claims that a sentence should be a "high energy construct and, at all points, an energy-discharge" (240). Ginsberg explains that he "use[s] [his] whole body" so that "poetry becomes [. . .] a physiological thing" (*Journals* 89–90). Ginsberg's poetics of breath and Olson's emphasis on energy evoke the "energy drives" that Kristeva finds in semiotic uses of language. In focusing on sentence constructions in relation to breathing, Olson and Ginsberg elucidate one of the ways in which the Semiotic can affect language. Through their emphasis on the speed, movement, motion, and change of breaths that "arrange the verse line on the page," Olson and Ginsberg reveal how poetry can formally perform semiotic drives ("Allen Ginsberg"). McElroy uses similar devices in prose and extends the trope of breath not only in relation to the page and line structure, as in Olson's and Ginsberg's works, but also to the semiotic rendering of Imp Plus's experience so that breath affects the content, rhythms, structure, and grammar of the text. In that sense, breath does not function as a mere formal device; it allows the body to be an integral part of writing.

Imp Plus's experience, when remembering having made love with a woman and progressively relearning the world through those tactile recollections, is congruent to the way the text is given a physical presence, breathing in and out:

> The California woman's hand had run a spiral ladder up his spine. Later she brought the small brown of her nipples up to him turn into one whole face then the loin of its open mouth then the multiplied nipplets of her velvet tongue: and all brought with them that desire that dissolved into its own unknown the fear of what was to come. (84)

The scene with the "California woman" starts with the repetition of the sound [h] in "hand," "had," and "his" in the first sentence. This sound involves a releasing of air and relates to breath. It is also the sound of heavy breathing, or breathlessness, which we can associate with exercise or sexual activity in this passage. The repetition of [ə] ("the," "California," "woman," "run," "a," spiral," and "up") and [æ] ("California," "had," and "ladder") adds a regular, breath-like rhythm to the text. Imp Plus plays with words whose sounds are close: "ladder" and "later," "brought" and "brown," which creates echoes and musical variations. The repetition of "then" also involves a rhythm in the sentence: when the reader first encounters "then," the sentence is longer through the accumulation of information. At that point, the rhythm of the sentence resembles the sentence of a child, accumulating ideas, whose story would never end. The repetition of "that" ("that desire that") furthers this effect, as does the lack of punctuation before "the fear of what was to come." As we cannot take a breath there, it feels as if the sentence accumulates too much information, in a rush, making us breathless. The lack of punctuation also blurs the meaning of the text: we have to slow down to understand the meaning of the sentence at that moment. As opposed to the fragmented breaths of the [h] sound in the first sentence, the second sentence elongates breathlessly.

McElroy's emphasis on breathing patterns, his exploration of the musicality of words, and his disruption of syntax are semiotic expressions. Thus, in the context of this study, *Plus* allows us to experience through semiotic plays with language the embodied mode of writing that *AVA, DICTEE,* and *VAS* explore through experiments with pagination, foreign languages, and visual texts. What is particularly interesting in *Plus*'s case is the semiotic practice it enables on a formal level and its questioning of the relationship between the Semiotic and Symbolic on a content level. Consequently, as a first step in this study, *Plus* allows us to experience an erotic language and reflect on how it appears in texts, as well as on the outcomes of its presence in reading and writing. Yet, it would be erroneous to conclude that Imp Plus transforms the Symbolic into a Semiotic realm. Rather, he is able to question the stability of the Symbolic from within, much like the Semiotic's revolutionary activities that reveal the flaws of the symbolic constancy in Kristeva's paradigm. As a result of this change, at the end of the novel, Imp Plus decides to conclude the experiment by coming closer to the sun, much like Icarus in the Greek myth, encountering

> some multiple twining that towered into headache, so he'd had to get to Sun and get to water. A twining in his head that primed what had been getting ready to happen. To happen whatever Earth did. To happen describable or not. He and the Sun described what happened. This describing was being. (204)

In deciding to come close to the sun he asks, "For was his growth not over? And was he not at the mercy of the being he had once become only then to lessen into a part of?" (206). Here, Imp Plus does not give in to the Symbolic. In the end, Imp Plus can continue to participate in the experiment, or "run away toward deep space," but "both of these options would mean accepting the patterns of instrumentalization and asocial empowerment the Powers-That-Be hope to incarnate in the cyborg body, whereas Imp Plus wants and needs connection and, above all, communication" (Proietti). His action can be interpreted as a refusal of the symbolic order, which limits his emotions and contains his semiotic experience.

Imp Plus's decision evokes Kristeva's words on the relationship between the body and linguistic structures:

> The human body is [. . .] a process. It is not a unity but a plural totality with separate members that have no identity but constitute the place where drives are applied. This dismembered body cannot fit together again, set itself in motion, or function biologically and physiologically, unless it is included within a practice that encompasses the signifying process.
>
> Without such practice, the body in process/on trial is disarticulated; its drives tear it up into stymied, motionless sectors and it constitutes a weighty mass. Outside the process, its only identity is inorganic, paralyzed, dead. (*Revolution* 101)

The experiment wants Imp Plus to become a machine. For Kristeva, this is the logical result of any system limited to the Symbolic. Similarly, Imp Plus sees this activity, deprived from signifying processes, as death, showing that the semiotic mode does not share a common structure with the Symbolic since the Semiotic relies on process and change. The scientists wish to deprive Imp Plus's communication of the Semiotic, which transforms his signifying process into machine-like inputs. However, Imp Plus's exploration of the Semiotic challenges the nature of the Symbolic because it explores process and change, not the stable measurements that Cap Com requires. This insistence on process and change implies that we also consider reading not as an input–output exchange, but rather, as we shall see more specifically in the following chapters, as a sensual interrelation that involves a mutual production of reader and text.

In *Plus,* such production relies on Imp Plus's refusal to become an instrument of the scientific experiment, which gives a material quality to language.

Instead of considering words as scientific codes that can neutrally measure and transmit biological data, Imp Plus allows words to grow a new body: "The two words held together like one thing—one quantity—apart from other things said; the two words had come to Imp Plus from any points like seabirds swinging into him over paths of spray till they were out of focus" (18). Commenting on this passage, McElroy asks:

> Is it a life made of words? More what they point to and secrete. Attach to, like hopes, like objects. Words together surprise. Phrases build. But what? Is it language discovered lost and found in fresh light. In self-defense is it? If there is a self; and if so, made of what? [. . .] The discoveries of this being Imp Plus, indeed of being Imp Plus, measure themselves by a progress of words, terms, modifiers like acts. In *Plus*, [. . .] growth is *embodied*. ("Plus Light")

Imp Plus's growth relies on his ability to build a new identity with words, using them like objects. Paradoxically, the body-less subject of McElroy's novel calls attention to the bodily urgency of this process, emphasizing the "parallel action in language and body" ("Plus *Light*"). Somehow, the thoughts going through Imp Plus's brain materialize in "limbs." Through this fantasy, McElroy stresses the materiality of language. Consequently, in *Plus,* he asks, "May not words be bodily?" or whether is it possible for "a body [to be] *thought* into being" and build "a new knowing, an *embodied* knowing whose source is hard to pin point" ("Plus *Light*"). McElroy's insistence on a bodily language alludes to the limits of scientific discourses that think of the body as a machine. This stress on embodiment allows us to think further about the relationship between science and the body without rejecting technology completely and without embellishing its effect on humans. The reconsideration of this relationship to knowledge establishes alternative knowing structures that link the body and language, and, as we shall see, Maso, Cha, and Tomasula also contribute to such structures.

The end of *Plus* clarifies the concept of *"embodied* knowing" since Imp Plus's suicide refuses both the thought that a human can be an instrument and the "mythologies of individual expansiveness" (Proietti). Because McElroy reveals that science and the senses are not distinct, the cyborg he creates in *Plus* is not reducible to a technological entity. In fact, as Yves Abrioux points out, the merging of science and senses allows for "muscular energy" to shape McElroy's prose, or what McElroy himself refers to as a "vectoral muscle" that offers "conjunctions of propulsion, motion, and poise, but equally of percept and affect as dynamic processes" (Abrioux 39). For Abrioux, this muscle "is not simply a handy metaphorical formulation alluding to the notion of cognitive embodiment [. . . .] It suggests a way out of abstractness," of what Leclair describes as systems, Hantke and Kuehl as demonstrations of conspiracy, and Tanner and Karl as topography (39). Abrioux explores the ways in which McElroy vectorizes his texts at different speeds and toward different directions, and concludes that the "repetitive and almost subliminal play on words," as well as "seemingly arbitrary conjunctions" and "disorientation," create "organic smoothness" in the novel (42, 51, 42, 49). In that sense, Abrioux's study of McElroy's fictions, like mine, emphasizes how *Plus*'s rhythms, sounds, and narrative structure, along with Imp Plus's defamiliarization of his environment and language, provide an embodied knowledge that emerges in our reading of the novel.

Abrioux's consideration of "muscular energy" and "vectoral muscle" also hints at another mode of embodiment, one that relies not on tactile sensibility but on proprioception. Proprioception, Massumi indicates, is "the sensibility proper to the muscles and ligaments" (58). As opposed to tactility, which relies on the skin's contact with another surface, proprioception "folds tactility into the body, enveloping the skin's contact with the external world" (58). In other words, the muscles and ligaments analyze and memorize the body's movements and reactions to surfaces. While proprioception is linked to the body's activity, in the context of *Plus* it can be considered as the muscular memory that "folds tactility in": Imp Plus's former limbs have registered how movement and surfaces feel (59). Proprioception's capacity to internalize external encounters results in an embodied knowledge where abstract and sensory, inside and outside, subject and object are inseparable: "Proprioceptive memory is where the infolded limits of the body meet the mind's externalized responses and where both rejoin the quasi corporeal and the event" (59). This reabsorption of tactility into the body illuminates the linguistic experiments of *Plus,* which attempt to bridge abstract and empirical, to find an in-between mode of expression where inside and outside interrelate.

This mode of expression leads us to discover, through our reading practice, a somatic dimension of the text which overrides the cognitive activity of understanding. As John Tambornino reminds us, "Appreciating the relation of language to corporeality underscores the *somatic effects* of writing, as a technique tapping into levels of thinking and being below the register of language. In conceiving of writing as a technique of the body, the linguistic and corporeal [. . .] converge" (137). In *Plus,* this somatic dimension implies that the deciphering of the text relies on a mutual formation of the reader and the text, which depends on a bodily mode of exchange. Such mode of exchange calls for a transformation of our reading habits and of our construction of knowledge, which Maso, Cha, and Tomasula clarify. In the context of McElroy's work, this somatic reading implies that the cybernetic approaches to his fictions overlook the connections between the body and cognitive mobility, interpreting McElroy's "vectoral muscle" as a mere technologization of human beings.

As Salvatore Proietti argues, *Plus* shows the limits of Nathan S. Kline and Manfred Clynes's 1960s cyborg theories. They proposed an

> epic narrative of mastery over the universe while ostensibly foregrounding a pluralism of embodiments, [and] posit[ed] not only a mechanistic view of the body, but also a faith and hope in its irrelevance and coming suppression: the self-regulating, homeostatic balance along the boundary of the interface between organic and inorganic components renders the cyborg less an empowered body than an armored mind. (Proietti)

I would extend Proietti's argument to cyborg theories beyond the 1960s, including Haraway's model. Indeed, for McElroy, technology does not bear the liberating prospect that cyborg theorists have emphasized in their exploration of the merging of technology and the body. On the contrary, McElroy criticizes explorations of the cyborg for oversimplifying the relationship between mind and body.

As I will show, this oversimplification is also true of our conception of New Media works. The use of technology in digital literature has raised questions about the freeing qualities of the digital medium, and also brought up the issue of the disappearance of the body along with the immateriality of information. Jonathan Crary, Paul Virilio, William Mitchell, and others have explored digital media's tendency to detach the viewer from an embodied sense of physical location. As Hayles shows, however, if we focus on the dematerialization of the body, we overlook "the *embodied* circumstances" that accompany this dematerialization (*How We Became* 193). Mark Hansen also draws our attention to the fact that embodiment "form[s] an integral part" of the digital: "embodiment is necessary to give it a place, to transform its endless self-differing into a concrete experience of today's informational (or 'post-medium') environment" (32). Like Hayles and Hansen, I find it more productive to construct an analytical framework that "integrate[s] the two camps of abstraction and embodiment" (*How We Became* 193). In this view, "As long as the human subject is envisioned as an autonomous self with unambiguous boundaries, the human–computer interface can only be parsed as a division between the solidity of real life on one side and the illusion of virtual reality on the other, thus obscuring the far-reaching changes initiated by the development of virtual technologies" (*How We Became* 291). *Plus*, in its exploration of the body and technology through embodied modes of knowledge, forecasts questions about the influence of technology on our reading practices and proposes an approach that avoids the division Hayles wishes to prevent.

McElroy's exploration of a new relationship between science and the human discloses the importance of embodiment and so reveals the limitations of Hantke's, Kuehl's, Leclair's, Tanner's, and Karl's readings. These critics overemphasize the abstract qualities of technology in McElroy's prose and fail to recognize his interest in hybrid structures that combine the human and the technological. In his essay "Neural Neighborhoods and Other Concrete Abstracts" (1974), McElroy made it clear that "in our life, dominant forces seem increasingly to depreciate the body and the emotions: yet inseparable from these forces are certain means of understanding that cannot be dismissed simply because their clarities are associated with what is called 'de-personalizing'" (206). Misreadings that overstress the sciences in McElroy's work as "de-personalizing" tools miss the complexity of his work, which problematizes myths about the role of science. What attracts McElroy to the sciences is that

> They're abstract in that they're generative models and modeling. Structures less fixed than in motion. Contained to a point, parallel to their elements and sources left visible and parallel to any discourse that might know and try to embody them, a passion-plotted anecdote, a geometric demonstration which might have its own body or sense appeal. ("Socrates" 10)

Consequently, readings that only address scientific systems in McElroy's work imply that the scientific interest in "generative models and modeling" is more important than its "passion-plotted anecdote[s]" and "sense appeal," and classify him as an advocate of discourses that view technological advancements as a salvation. In breaking down the boundaries that these critiques maintain between science and pleasure, McElroy allows us to practice the lack of boundaries that Kristeva, Deleuze and Guattari, or Lecercle theorize. In *Plus*, the *jouissance* that comes from this experience reinforces the importance of the body in our use of language. Thus, the novel's scientific vocabulary is surprisingly an erotic invitation to explore language, and the novel's construction of a hybrid body allows us to understand what is at stake in the libidinal traces in language. In other words, *Plus* enables us to practice "*embodied* knowing," which leads us not only to reevaluate language paradigms that repress the Semiotic, as Kristeva claims, but also to engage our bodies in our knowing practice.

Therefore, *Plus* enables the reader to experience an erotic reading, one that breathes in and out of the text. Through the allegorical representations of the Semiotic and Symbolic, the rhythms, and syntactic and grammatical disruptions, the novel both theorizes and practices *jouissance*. This verbal bliss relies on the use of technology and complex structures in McElroy's work. The novel thus allows a communication with the complexities of our hypertechnological world, a communication full of the erotics and sensuality of our daily experiences. Technology and sensuality are not opposed in McElroy's novels, and this connection changes the reader's approach to fiction, inviting an erotics of reading. After the reading of *Plus,* then, it becomes clear that an erotics of language starts with the dissolution of boundaries and of a centered self. In *AVA,* such dissolutions directly engage the medium of the text because the fragmentation and typographical spacing of Maso's text provide another erotic encounter with language.

chapter three

"A Certain Pulsing"

THE EROTIC PAGE IN CAROLE MASO'S *AVA*

> You are beautiful
>
> forgetting any of the important parts.
>
> How is this for a beginning?
>
> There is scarcely a day that goes by that I do not think of you.
>
> Turn over on your side.

FIGURE 6. Carole Maso. *AVA* p. 8 (c) 1993 Dalkey Archive Press.

AVA recounts the last day of Ava Klein, a thirty-nine-year-old professor of comparative literature, who is dying of a rare cancer. Thus, the recollection of her thoughts, as exemplified in this passage, is often interrupted by medical requests—"Turn over on your side" (8). Here, it is unclear whether a nurse or doctor utters this sentence while Ava thinks of her life; it could also be part of a scene that she remembers, just like she remembers someone beautiful. Or maybe someone used to tell her that she was beautiful. Perhaps one of her lovers would tell her, "There is scarcely a day that goes by that I do not think of you," or Ava may have told her lover so (8). The difficulty of attributing these sentences to a clear context is in line with the narrative's fragmented rendering of key themes that wander through the protagonist's mind—her miscarriage, the books she taught, her lovers and her three husbands, her family's experience of the Holocaust, her travels in Europe, and so forth—on August 15, 1990, the day of Iraq's invasion of Kuwait. These thoughts are separated into three sections—morning, afternoon, and night—but the narration is made up of fragmented memories of Ava's life, quotes, interviews, and letters that do not form a coherent whole.

According to Maso, what is important is that, in reading *AVA*, "there are things that are there that would be a common journey. The fact that it is a journey is one of those things; and that it is indeterminate, and simultaneously there seems to be a holding on and a letting go" (personal interview). While *AVA* may not construct a narrative that logically and linearly builds toward a resolution of the plot, the novel is set up so that each reader will participate in combining the fragments of Ava's life, and so will go on a journey. Maso qualifies this journey as indeterminate because the text does not dictate a specific progression through the book. This is particularly apparent when *AVA*'s narrator quotes Rosemarie Waldrop on Edmond Jabès in *Epoch*: "Shifting voices and constant breaks of mode let silence have its share and allow for a fuller meditative field than is possible in linear narrative or analysis" (184). Therefore, the fragmentation and white breaks of the novel are meant to create an "indeterminate journey," allowing the reader to meditate simultaneously the possibilities of life and of literature.

Like Ava's first husband Francesco, Maso "make[s] no apologies for [her text's] seemingly random format (it is not)" (152). Indeed, the text is not random; it is "seemingly random" in order to challenge our uses of language and narrative patterns. For example, comments on composition in the above excerpt—"forgetting any of the important parts. / How is this for a beginning?"—playfully interrupt the associative thought process of Ava (8). While these remarks may be part of Ava's composition of her memories, they also figure at the beginning of the book, thereby commenting on its compositional strategies. Indeed, *AVA* self-consciously acknowledges the artifice of fiction writing by inviting the reader to ponder literary conventions and become "no longer a consumer, but a producer of the text" (*S/Z* 4). In presenting Ava's situation this way, Maso disrupts linguistic and narrative structures and insists on the physicality of the page, which expresses the desires of an erotic body. This approach to writing has often been understood as the development of a feminist mode of storytelling.

Indeed, Maso's novels use unconventional forms to tell the stories of women in relation to language, art, memory, sexuality, and gender. *Ghost Dance* (1986) deals with the struggles of Vanessa Turin, as she attempts to recover her family and her past. In *The Art Lover* (1990), Caroline, a novelist and poet, reflects on the relationship between life and art as she rediscovers New York City after a writing retreat. The novel combines reproductions of pictures and newspaper clippings, as they interrelate with

Caroline's life, her characters', as well as that of a friend diagnosed with AIDS. In *The American Woman in the Chinese Hat* (1994), Catherine, a bisexual writer, relates her experiences in France as she goes through various sexual encounters. *Aureole* (1996) is an erotic novel about an American woman coming to terms with her sexuality. *Defiance* (1998) focuses on physics professor Bernadette O'Brien, who is in prison after murdering two students. Awaiting execution, she writes her life story, interrelating her passion for mathematics with childhood stories, sexual fantasies, and reflections on death row. In *Beauty Is Convulsive: The Passion of Frida Kahlo* (2002), Maso investigates Kahlo's mental and physical struggles. In her novels, Maso's exploration of female characters through formal innovation relies on "an experience that exists as heat or light, friction, dissolution, as spirit, as body, as a world that overflows the covers of the book, and crosses into a kind of derangement, a kind of urgency, waywardness, need—a pulsing, living, strange thing" (*Rain Taxi*). Maso's approach to language asks that we reconsider our relationship to words, as they become part of an embodied approach to language and knowledge.

Maso explores this embodied mode in the sonic associations of *AVA*. As Lucia Cordell Getsi notes, "There is something both gravitational and gestational in the way the phrases and lines of the novel—repeating in bits, repeating in wholes or parts, not repeating sometimes—go about their work, in the ways we communicate, which is not the way novels, even other experimental novels, even lyric novels, communicate." The narrative repeats key phrases—"you are a rare bird," "Samuel Beckett on a tree," "We were working on an erotic song cycle." These iterations create sonic associations, through the repetition, for example, of the name "Ana Julia" and through the linkage of the sound "[a]" found in other nouns in the same page, "Tia Dora," "mama," "Blanquita," and "milagro" (39). Such thematic and sonic variations render bodily fluxes and rhythms, constructing refrains for "songs the blood sings" (59). Hence, the originality Getsi stresses in Maso's work relies on the way it invites us to a physical engagement with *AVA*. According to Maso, *AVA* is a text concerned with "space, temporal and shape relations, tone and tempo. [Lyrical novels] are sensitive to tensions and pulls, resistances—gatherings and release" (*Break* 33). The reader's response to such gatherings and releases is physical because, as Barbara Page proposes, "the rhythmic succession of passages induces a condition approaching trance" (Page par. 90). Page refers here to the ways in which Maso's use of formal devices—repetitions, sonic variations, stress patterns, and fragmentation—does not attempt to represent Ava's changing condition, but allows the reader to feel it.

This way of expressing Ava's life renders what Barthes refers to as the "un-sayable" qualities of texts of *jouissance*. Such texts invite readers to rely on the materiality of language—not on representation—to explore linguistic bliss.[1] For Barthes, blissful texts feature "a perpetual interweaving; lost in this tissue—this texture—the subject unmakes himself, like a spider dissolving in the constructive secretions of its web" (*Pleasure* 64). This unmaking of the subject is akin to Ava's "interweaving" identity. Through her "*hyphos*" ("the tissue and the spider's web"), Ava "unmakes" herself, and creates a fluid identity (64). Such unmaking occurs when Ava mentions events happening during the Holocaust. Because of the fragmentation and elusiveness of the novel, it may seem as though she confuses her life with those of other women who experienced extermination camps. Her memory of the camps goes back to her family history: Ava is the only child of Philip and Rachel Klein, survivors of Treblinka. Ava mentions that "They were left to the left," and refers to "Piles of hair" (25, 245). She also recalls Sophie, Rachel's sister, who was shot, "pleading in front of the great pit for her life"; the death of Sophie's parents; and that of her homosexual brother Sol (72).

However, when Ava remembers details from her family's life, she sometimes presents them as if she took part in them. For example, we read, "At the gas chamber, when I was chosen to work there as a barber, some of the women that came in on a transport were from my town" (111). At the end of the novel, Maso "attribute[s] the sources of [the] 'irresistible music'" of Ava's "passionate and promiscuous reading," and she notes that this sentence is taken from Lanzmann's *Shoah*. Yet, when we read it without referring to the "sources" page of the novel, we may identify the "I" with Ava (269). Because Maso's "hope is that [the] notes, at some point, will enhance the reader's pleasure but in no way interrupt the trance of the text," we are invited, when we are in this "trance," to make connections between the porous identities of the characters (269).

According to Barthes, such fluid identities engage "a 'living contradiction': a split subject, who simultaneously enjoys [. . .] the consistency of his selfhood and its collapse, its fall" (*Pleasure* 21). Ava embodies this "living contradiction," as she both celebrates life while dying—repeating "I want to live" and "I am dying"—and takes pleasure in the fragmenting connec-

---

1. My theoretical choice may appear contradictory to Maso's project here, as Maso claims to be influenced by Cixous, whom she also quotes throughout *AVA*. While I do not deny that Cixous's work has affinities with the novel, I contend that Barthes provides comments on writing in relation to the "un-sayable" that are more useful than Cixous's, and that allow us to reconsider the relationship between Maso's and Cixous's works. In addition, Barthes's comments bear a resemblance to Maso's goals in the novel, because in writing *AVA*, she tried to be "at the reach of the things that can't really be said" (personal interview).

tions of her mind while her disease partly causes this fragmentation. There is a tension between Ava's wish to rely on the consistency of her selfhood, to insist on her uniqueness, while also negating it when branching into other women's lives and enjoying these disruptions of the cohesiveness of her life. For example, she mentions "Shiny hair on the pillow next to me: it was mine and not mine," and states, "It is and is not my body" (61, 128). As Karen Lee Osborne points out, "Ava's character is as multiple, fluid, and open-ended as the many separate moments she remembers or imagines." This implies that while Ava constructs her memories and builds a rendition of her life, she at the same time destroys it. A similar unmaking of Ava occurs when Maso uses the pronoun "she" but does not clearly relate it to a specific person. In turn, "she" stands for Ava, her aunt, her mother, Virginia Woolf, and other influential female figures in Ava's life, making it impossible to clearly identify who is performing the action. As Maso points out, this lack of centered identity applies directly to the reading experience of *AVA*.

Maso's use of a permeable identity for her character interrelates with the fragmentation method, which forces the reader to wander, like Ava, in various contexts:

> The attempt in *AVA* is that narrative motifs might produce a design of images. To interweave motifs through the text by use of recurrences, repetitions, etc., which often act contrapuntally and trigger through theme, rhythm, and other mysterious methods associations in the reader as well as the writer. Often it is the act itself, the association-making process rather than the subject, that is recognizable. (*Break* 38)

Maso insists on the "association-making process" that enables the depiction of a fluid identity and encourages readers to identify not with a centered character evolving in a specific context but with a more open identity. Here, her goal is close to McElroy's in presenting a non-*thetic* subject. Thus, as the study of *Plus* and *AVA* reveals, an erotics of language relies on a discontinuous self.

In *AVA,* this erotic process occurs when the reader feels enmeshed in the weaving of the fragmented remembrance of Ava's life. Through this immersion in the rhythms and textures of words, readers come closer to the textual medium, losing their sense of self (see figure 7). In the following passage, it is impossible to know whose "bellies" the narrator is talking about or where the scene takes place exactly—"Fourteenth Street" is mentioned earlier, but this is the only location mentioned. We are unable to rely on a conceptualization of what this moment was like and what happened, and we cannot

> Salsa floats down from a high-up apartment.
>
> Their bellies which are vermillion. And the word *vermillion*.
>
> She finds herself on a foreign coast on her thirty-third birthday.

FIGURE 7. Carole Maso. *AVA* p. 65 (c) 1993 Dalkey Archive Press.

identify with specific characters. Instead, we focus on the words, their connections, and sounds: the association of the color red with "salsa" and "vermillion" and the play on "up" and "down" force us to concentrate on the sonorities and connotations of words, not just on what they refer to. What "and the word *vermillion*" really means remains unclear, but the italics call our attention to the way the word itself feels. This attention paid to the linguistic material of the text follows Ava's "determin[ation] to reshape the world according to the dictates of desire—" (6).

These "dictates of desire" engage textual loss, rapture, discomfort, and shock. The novel does not satisfy the reader's wish to follow a train of thought by reading a sentence until it ends, nor does it satisfy the reader's wish to assemble elements of the protagonist's life into a narration. Maso's paratactic syntax relies not on customary narrative and grammatical continuity but on fragmentation and polysemy, which, for Ron Silliman, participate in the formation of a "new sentence." According to him, "new sentences" are crafted so that their connection or independence remains unspecified. This unfixed mode of signification, or what he calls "torquing," makes meaning relational and unstable because the disjointed fragments, while not subordinated to a larger frame or logic, affect and question each other. In other words, the arrangement of the "new sentence" is not random, and, as the following example shows, the locus of tension between sentences is meaningful:

> Yes, I am positive, he said, that day in the snow. Holding Italian magazines in the street.
>
> For some time no one was sure whether or not the war had ended.
>
> A pot au feu, in cold weather. By the fire.
>
> Breathe.
>
> Close up you are exactly like a statue.
>
> The child draws the letter A.

FIGURE 8. Carole Maso. *AVA* p. 44 (c) 1993 Dalkey Archive Press.

It is impossible to know whether the man in this passage is certain about something or whether he has contracted HIV (see figure 8). We can infer this reference to AIDS since the disease is mentioned earlier. Later on, we discover that Aldo's lover, Andrew, has "tested positive for the AIDS virus" (200). Aldo's answer to the question "Are you positive?" is "Yes, I am extremely positive. [. . .] In fact, I've got the first signs—forgetfulness, night sweats" (99). The use of the adverb "extremely" seems to exclude a reference to AIDS, as "extremely positive" is a commonplace collocation. However, Aldo's allusion to "forgetfulness" and "night sweats" reveals that "extremely" means "terminally" in this case. The delayed inference contributes to the sense of blur the text induces. On page 44, before we can clarify the statement "Yes, I am positive," we move on to a sentence about the war, and because Ava has mentioned the Gulf War and the Second World War, we are unsure about the context of this statement.

Nevertheless, semantic connections lead us toward a cohesive reading of this passage. "Positive" and "sure" connect semantically. Also, "feu" echoes "fire" in "A pot au feu, in cold weather. By the fire." These sentences may relate to the first statement in this passage since snow was mentioned, but it is not certain, especially since the "pot au feu," a traditional French dish, may be associated with Ava's life in France, which does not logically correlate to the "Italian magazines." As a result, these clues are only partial, so that it is impossible to draw conclusions from them: one could eat a "pot au feu" or read "Italian magazines" in any country. "Breathe" interrupts the recollection of the fire snapshot, and the next thought, "close up you are exactly like a statue," describes an unknown character, or it may be a sentence Ava heard about herself. The connection to the child's activity is left unclear. Hence, the text does not follow an apparent and logical pattern to present Ava's life; instead it roots our reading in a lack of information and transition. We thus realize that the semantic connections we initially expected to lead us to comprehend the story of Ava only participate in the weaving textures of Maso's fiction. The organization of information requires that we "fill in the blanks" (43).

The novel's use of references and direct citations from Lorca, Eliot, Beckett, Boltanski, Goethe, Danto, Woolf, Celan, Blake, Stevens, Sappho, Nin, Wittig, Cixous, O'Hara, Dickinson, Hesse, and others accentuates such blank-filling activity and creates connections between Ava's life and that of prominent writers. While blurring Ava's words with those of other writers, Maso also introduces a rupture between these works and hers, thus displacing, subverting, and playing with her references. In doing so, she "reconstruct[s] [. . . ,] critique[s], *create*[s] a 'surplus'" (Moraru 21). For

Christian Moraru, "Textual production through 'inserts,' intertextual 'graft-
ings,' and retellings ironically [. . .] activates [. . .] cultural appropriation and reincorporation" (132). In *AVA*, such "reincorporation" occurs
at multiple levels of interpretation: the quotes might be attributed to Ava's
memories of her comparative literature readings; they are also what constructs the remembrance of her life now that her body and consciousness are
breaking down. In some ways, they also "reincorporat[e]" Ava's body, while
also comprising the body of the text. As we shall see, this double construction allows readers to focus not only on Ava's life but also on the interstices
between her sentences and other writers', just as one focuses on a "*body
where the garment gapes?*" (*Pleasure* 9).

For Barthes, this mode of reading plays with our desire but does not
satisfy it, and this leads to *jouissance*. Hence, our ecstatic state relies not
on the fulfillment of our wish to understand Ava's life but on a lack or loss;
it is always fleeting, displaced, empty, and unpredictable (*Pleasure* 21). In
other words, while it may be tempting, at first, to try and reach a cohesive
interpretation of the fragmentary novel, we soon realize that this tempta-
tion is more important than is the goal of interpreting *AVA* holistically. As
R. M. Berry notes, the fragmented text may seem inaccessible because it
may be holistic in Ava's mind only. On the other hand, we may associate
our reading with a puzzle-solving activity, which implies that we have the
ability to make sense of the story. Yet, the power of the novel may actually
lie in the fact that the fragments cannot be connected in our mind or in
Ava's:

> If we say the fragments are connected by or in Ava's consciousness, we will
> be interpreting what connects them, not describing it, and saying that they
> are not connected, that the reader must connect them, only confuses the
> issue: first, by suggesting that the reader could just do this, as if we knew
> some way of connecting the fragments of *AVA* that did not raise the same
> problems as *AVA* itself, and second, by suggesting that the reader could
> *not* do it, that we knew some way of reading *AVA without* connecting its
> fragments. [. . .] [I]f in order to be complete reading must presuppose a
> finality impossible of rearrangement, then the reader's plight is as hopeless
> as Ava's. (Berry 124)

Berry exposes the paradoxical situation that Maso's use of fragments provokes. In underlying the "finality impossible of rearrangement," he evokes
Barthes's definition of perverse texts, which "are outside of any imaginable finality" (*Pleasure* 52). However, Berry associates *AVA*'s finality with

the hopeless situation of its protagonist, and concludes, "no single life will exhaust life; no text will comprehend the meaningful" (124). On the contrary, for Barthes, "flirtatious texts" such as *AVA* constitute a perverse revealing of information, which leads to an erotic satisfaction (*Pleasure* 6). While I do not disagree with Berry's assessment, I contend that there is not only hopelessness but also pleasure coming from the "perverse" organization of *AVA*.

In Maso's novel, this organization plays with our desire for direct access to Ava's life. Momentary dissolutions of meaning require that, instead of assembling moments of her life in order to achieve a larger and more complete story, we focus on bits of life, unfinished stories, elusive leads, and silence. In that sense, the fragmentation of the text comes between our wish for a direct approach to Ava's story, and, in playing with our wishes, it disperses our desire in another direction—the material medium of the novel. The dissemination of meaning enables the reader to approach the text differently, without focusing on its meaning only, since the latter has obliterated into multiple contexts. Instead, the reader can enjoy a perverse reading, one that plays with the content and medium of the text. The perverse reader usurps the communicative goal of his or her reading and takes pleasure in his or her playful approach to the text.

For Barthes, this mode of reading brings text and body closer: "Does the text have human form, is it a figure, an anagram of the body? Yes, but of our erotic body" (*Pleasure* 17). Barthes's use of the concept of the anagram implies that, in order to be legible, a text needs a material support or a discursive body. He adds, "the text itself, a diagrammatic and not an imitative structure, can reveal itself in the form of a body, split into fetish objects, into erotic sites" (*Pleasure* 56). However, just as the everyday uses of our bodies are not erotic, our basic uses of language for daily communication are not blissful. Thus, Barthes insists on associating the *erotic* qualities of the body with textuality because bodily pleasures associated with physiological needs relate to pornography more than eroticism. What writings of the "*inter-dit*" explore erotically is not the representation of intercourse but the inexpressibility of bodily passions. Consequently, both the erotic text and the erotic body are bliss materials because they play with desire: they do not represent it or imitate it, but they show it through figuration.

According to Barthes, figuration relies on a linguistic excess that allows the reader to "lea[p] out of the frame" of the story (*Pleasure* 57). The text, as it avoids representation, which Barthes qualifies as an "*embarrassed figuration*, encumbered with other meanings than that of desire: a space of alibis," can access the figuration of Eros (*Pleasure* 56). In describing and dissecting the object of desire, representation lacks the fleeting qualities of *jouissance*. On the other hand, the erotic body and the texts of the "*interdit*" express these qualities through excess. In other words, the erotic body/ text does not tell its blissful experiences, nor does it imitate its desire for it. Instead, it plays with it.[2] In Barthes's work, playful uses of language rely on the paradoxical role of figuration, which both "figures" and "de-figures." In revealing the inexpressible, figuration relies on an intermittence of appearance and disappearance; it reveals as much as it obscures.

Barthes clarifies this intermittence in his writing on photography. His use of the photographic media is no incident, as the concept of overexposure relates to the figuration process: when a photograph is overexposed, although it becomes white, it does not represent a void but bears the mark of the light it has caught. This revealing and concealing dynamic in photography illuminates the (de)figuration process in language. Both the literary and photographic media can reveal and obscure through figuration: images are created "thanks to figuration," but what comes through it, traverses it, is also part of the figuration process. For Barthes, this figuration process takes the reader and the viewer outside the frame of the artwork:

> Pornography ordinarily represents the sexual organs, making them into a motionless object [. . .]. The erotic photograph, on the contrary (and it is its very condition), does not make the sexual organs into a central object; it may very well not show them at all; it takes the spectator outside its frame, and it is there that I animate this photograph and that it animates me. (*Camera* 58–59)

According to Barthes, this animation is possible because his experience of the visual is tactile.

Rather than insisting on the distance between the photograph and himself, Barthes proposes to focus on embodied methods of interpretation. To develop this tactile method for reading photography, Barthes relies on the concept of *punctum*. The *punctum* is the detail or portion of a photograph that "rises from the scene, shoots out of it like an arrow, and pierces" the viewer (26). The *punctum* catches the viewer's attention by accident and "pricks" and "bruises" him or her (43). Barthes's use of metaphors reveals that the *punctum* is tactile and induces movement. In that sense, it triggers a

---

2. This excess in Barthes's model resembles Kristeva's Semiotic. Barthes's and Kristeva's works on the sensual uses of language are close, but here Barthes insists on the playful uses of linguistic processes, which can be compared to sexual foreplay, while Kristeva locates the sexual origins of the Semiotic in repressed libidinal drives.

deep corporeal connection with the photographic material. This fusion with the artistic medium allows an erotic approach to art.

In Maso's text, the *punctum* lies in the reader's escape from the representational mode to engage in linguistic foreplay. In other words, the reader does not focus strictly on the message the text conveys but focuses also on the textual material of *AVA*. He or she comes close to the page of the text, its white space and its plays with the meanings and connotations of words. In that sense, "*AVA* does not demand interpretation. It demands engagement and enactment and a spiraling up out of the deep shaft of associations into the spacious white markers that weave their silence through syntagmatic canvas and wait for the reader to chime in with a resonance from the well of the paradigmatic, the core (heart) of the self" (Getsi). Thus, the text does not simply deliver a message but absorbs the reader through linguistic excess. Maso explains how her project employs a physical language that calls for such engagement from the reader:

I have tried to get closer to an erotic language, a language that might function more bodily, more physically, more passionately. Enjambment, flux, fragmentation, the elision of the object, the detached clause, the use of arpeggios, a changing of dynamics, dangling participles, various aphasias— the unfinished sentence, or the melting of one sentence into another, the melting of corporeal boundaries, the dissolving of subjective cohesion— these are some of the strategies I have attempted. [. . .] For the most part they were done intuitively as I tried to surrender and enter a sexual reverie on the level of language. (*Break* 118)

In experimenting with forms, Maso brings her text closer to the workings of an erotic body, one that dissolves and melts with another, and one that longs in desire through "elisions," detachment, changes, and surprises. Her goal is close to McElroy's in *Plus,* as Imp Plus and Ava both take pleasure in the linguistic medium they utilize to express themselves. While both characters use language in an unusual way to express parts of their lives that are unsayable, the causes for such sensual linguistic issues are quite different: *Plus* relies on the science fiction premise that the brain is detached from its body and grows new limbs through memories, and Ava is remembering her life on her deathbed. However, in both works, the fragments of one's life and the erotic drives that penetrate language change the narrative and linguistic structures of the novels. Let us consider such instances in *AVA* (see figure 9). *AVA* is full of surprises, mixing the poetic mood of the earth's "blue blanket" with the conversational "Zinnias are always nice" (251). Such

Small earth in its blanket of blue.

Broken sky.

I love you.

Flowers in danger

Zinnias are always nice

Love in the hallucinatory afternoon.

A helmet.

Ocean of blood.

FIGURE 9. Carole Maso. *AVA* p. 251 (c) 1993 Dalkey Archive Press.

surprises play with our interpretive process and our desire to make sense of the text.

The white space that separates the lines teases us in another way: the rhythms that the white spaces mark are like "orgasm, [. . .] like a little death, an escape from ordinary time" (Osborne). In the above passage, each break in the text creates a rhythm of silence that, like orgasm, "disrupts time and disconnects us from words and being" (Osborne). We thus approach "the zone of speechlessness one sometimes enters during sex, the field of silence, the tug of it, the language voids and vacuums, the weird filling in with words" (*Break* 118). It is through this orgasmic connection to the silence of the text that we come close to Ava in her dying state. Therefore, while one may interpret Ava's death as a lack of life, in her acceptance of her own disappearance, she exposes the power of the seemingly empty sections of life and writing.

Maso's use of white spaces expands onto the ostensibly vacant parts of the page. In her insistence on the physicality of the page, Maso exposes a dimension of fiction different from McElroy's work. Indeed, she invites us to extend our sensual relationships to texts in our engagement with both language and textual materiality. In her novel, textual materiality tackles the issue of inexpressibility, as the white spaces avoid representation (i.e., the moment "when nothing emerges, when nothing leaps out of the frame: of the picture, the book, the screen") (Barthes *Pleasure* 57). Maso tackles this "leap out of the frame" in her novel:

You feel at the altar of the un-sayable. [. . .] For me, *AVA* is the book that gets closest to that, because it's all about the things that I can't really say and that I don't know how to say and that only are said in the ways that the lines relate to one another. They can be said straightforwardly by reading the thing in whatever way you read it. And for me, in writing it, I could not write it in any other way. So that kind of reach seemed to me the most important thing. (personal interview)

In *AVA*, this "reach" toward the "un-sayable" takes place not only in language but also in the use of white space that separates the lines of the text. In other words, Maso explores the "un-sayable" by allowing the lines to relate openly so that the un-written text carries, perhaps, the most important text of the novel. This implies not that the lines themselves are unimportant, but that their exploration of the "un-sayable" lies in their ability to connect.

Thus, *AVA* gives access to the "un-sayable" and the "*inter-dit*" because it is an in-between text that undertakes the paradox of expressing the inexpressible. With the phrase "*inter-dit*," Barthes plays on the words "*interdit*" (forbidden) and "*inter-dit*" (said between). The mode of the "*inter-dit*" is between two forms of expression: silence and language. This mode is forbidden because of its hybrid nature, which implicitly disrupts the accepted binary structure expressivity relies on. The fleeting aspect of the linguistic bliss paradoxically relies on a language that materializes experiences and thoughts that only exist in a displaced and differed mode. Hence, the text of *jouissance* is in-between; it relies on the "sayable" through its use of language, and challenges the expressibility of language, as it ventures to use language to convey the "un-sayable."

Conversely, in trying to represent the unrepresentable, Maso does not aim at transcendence outside the text, nor is she expressing a mere void. In *AVA*, the "un-sayable" manifests, not as a lack of communication, but instead as an excess of communication. Hence, Maso etches out a narrative that ruptures closure in its exploration of the "*inter-dit*" so that her text "allows the possibility for the most abstract of reflections: The limits of language" (Berlin). Consider this reflection in the following passage (see figure 10). The text does not clarify what was meant to be said. The shift from the restaurant scene to the theme of pregnancy, which introduces a poetic collage of fertile and fruitful tropes, expresses the "un-sayable" situation of Ava on her deathbed. She is dying, and the fractured and associative mode of recollections attempt to enact her need to stretch out time and hold on to life. Such moments lead to an "intermittence" that activates an erotic mechanism. In fragmenting the lines and using the white material of the text, Maso gives presence to an un-written narrative. In this sense, her text, as an "*inter-dit*," should literally be read between the lines. She explores the

> What I wanted to say—what I meant to say—the other night at the restaurant.
>
> Where I looked up to the sky and wept.
>
> Speak to me.
>
> She's very pregnant
>
> Orange and mimosa groves.
>
> And under the pomegranate. . . .

FIGURE 10. Carole Maso. *AVA* p. 85 (c) 1993 Dalkey Archive Press.

"intermittence," the in-between material, but does not express "un-sayable" emotions, avoiding representation. Thus, the text exists as much in the lines of words as in the visible seams that enable torquing. As Silliman notes, sentences such as Maso's "revea[l] that the blank space, between words or sentences, is much more than the 27th letter of the alphabet. [The new sentence] is beginning to explore and articulate just what those hidden capacities might be" (92). This revelation of white expanses reclaims the space that would normally express a break in or the end of a text. Instead of symbolizing such interruption or closure, white spaces introduce a new hierarchy between the materials and frames of fiction: they become "a force, against which the whole must be recovered, or against which the whole can be fractured, dissolved, let go" (Drucker *Figuring* 140). However, this white force does not negate or alienate the power of words: Maso's goal is not to destroy narration.

Indeed, Maso explains, "I feel slightly perplexed I must say when I hear *AVA* is not narrative. I think it just redefines narrative, reformulates it" (*Rain Taxi*). Because death is the focus and motif of *AVA*, the question of closure becomes important on a thematic and formal level. In other words, Ava's struggle to live mirrors the form of the novel, which constantly skirts closure. This evasion elicits a reconsideration of fragmentation and white spaces. In the novel, we read: "Artist's statement: I certainly admire many narrative and documentary films, but instead of re-creating or reproducing a familiar world it's been more exciting to collect an odd assortment of images, both scripted and shot from real life" (224). While this statement expresses an opinion about films and narratives, it relates directly to *AVA*, whose narration also "collects[s] an odd assortment of images, both scripted and shot from real life." For Maso, this collage technique allows a reformulation of narrative conventions and enables her to explore the in-between-ness of narratives—the link between silence and words.

Ava herself explores this connection: "Sing me a wordless song," she commands (151). She reassures Francesco, "Much is expressed in the interval. Do not worry so much about our silences when they come. I hear you even then," and states that she "can usually hear where the line is breaking" (248, 136). Her phrasing is paradoxical, since the break of the line is a moment of silence. Hence, in insisting on the paradox of this aural activity, Ava implies that there is more to the silence of the white spaces than just emptiness. A paragraph on Sarraute confirms this interpretation: "the genuine response to art is on an immediate and personal level. It is essentially a wordless conversation between the author and the reader" (61). This statement comments on the "wordless" material of *AVA*. Through the constant disjuncture of thoughts pointing to the white spaces that separate them, the novel calls attention to the discrepancy between words and meaning, and alludes to the "un-sayable" qualities of the text. Indeed, as Robin Silbergleid points out, "Maso's book is [. . .] fundamentally about those spaces between, about the relationship between the said and the unsaid, the author and the reader, the pleasure, and the weight of silence" (3).

In drawing attention to the disjunction between syntactical units, the white spaces thus become indices of their material cause, which is to say the page. In that sense, Maso's use of white spaces in *AVA* compares to the use of white canvas in visual arts, which visual art critics—Barthes, Didi-Huberman, J. M. Bernstein, J. T. Clark, W. J. T. Mitchell, Drucker, and Jeremy Gilbert-Rolfe—have explored. Visual art critics refer to the part of an artwork that is left blank, that appears in painting, underneath the paint, as reserve. The reserve is particularly important in impressionist or contemporary paintings, as in Cézanne's or Pollock's work, where the canvas is not a surface to be merely covered with paint but becomes part of the composition of the painting. In *AVA*, the white spaces, much like a painting's reserve, are not meant to be covered by words. Instead, they are part of the composition of Ava's life. The term "reserve" further qualifies the white spaces' role in the novel, as the word denotes "reticence" and "shyness," as well as "storage." The polysemy of the concept of reserve applies to the ways in which Maso uses white spaces because instead of arresting the text, they reveal the materiality of the book, which is usually "stored" by traditional reading techniques. In that sense, the white reserve allows us to reconsider the materiality of writing.[3] More specifi-

---

3. For a detailed study of the relationship between reserve and writing, see Marc

cally, this attention to textual materiality relates to the *pan* in the images Didi-Huberman studies.

Both the *pan* and the white spaces exceed representation. In Vermeer's *The Lacemaker*, a flow of red paint escapes from the sewing box as a wild tangle of red thread, which "creates a burst of color in the foreground of the work" (251). For Didi-Huberman, the "*pan* of red paint [in Vermeer's *Lacemaker*] unsettles, even tyrannizes, the representation. For it is imbued, this *pan*, with a singular capacity for expansion and diffusion: it infects, we might even say affects [. . .] the entire picture" (256). When we see the red stain, we are forced to stop focusing on the scene Vermeer painted because the *pan* of color does not represent anything and does not add an element that fits with the rest of the scene. Instead, it calls attention to its materiality—the color and the grain of the paint. Modernist painters have foregrounded such use of color and grain, the "paint-stuff (pigment)," which in the works of Soutine, for example, reveals that "in art the medium is not a neutral vehicle for the expression of an otherwise immaterial meaning, but rather the very condition for sense-making" (Bernstein 75).

Because this use of paint, like the white space in *AVA*, is not representational, it calls attention to itself as a nondecodable trace. The *pan* and the white space in *AVA* do not "fit" with the represented entities, but they refer to their medium and identify the paradox of their existence. Thus, the "*pan* [. . .] imposes itself, in the picture, like an accident of representation—of representation delivered up to the risk of the material paint. It is in this sense that the '*pan*' of paint imposes itself in the picture, simultaneously as accident of representation (*Vorstellung*) and sovereignty of presentation (*Darstellung*)" (Didi-Huberman 259–260). As T. J. Clark points out, in Modernist works, such as Cezanne's, the application of paint that does not fit traditional representational methods, as in the *pan*, "gives glimpses of alternative systems of representation" that "are less interesting in their own right [. . .] than as *repoussoir* for the system they still belong to. They are what makes that system visible as such" (165). Hence, these "alternative systems of representation" work against traditional modes of representation: they show their limits and inadequacies. Yet, these nontraditional painting methods also reveal what traditional modes of painting are in the first place: they expose what we took for granted in representational painting. Thus, as W. J. T. Mitchell proposes, instead of concentrating on representation or its negation, it might be more suitable to consider representation as "a multidimensional and heterogeneous terrain, a collage or patchwork quilt

Chénetier's *Sgraffites, encres & sanguines.*

[. . .] torn, folded, wrinkled, covered with accidental stains, traces of the bodies it has enfolded" (419). Considering representation this way "would make materially visible the structure of representation as a trace of temporality and exchange, the fragment as mementos, as 'presents' re-presented in the ongoing process of assemblage, of stitching in and tearing out" (419). This quilt-like understanding of representation implies that representation is not as much an object as it is "a kind of activity, process, or set of relationships" (420). This conception reveals that "What lies 'beyond' representation would thus be found 'within' it [. . .] or along its margins" (419). Mitchell's views are illuminating in the context of Maso's work because they immerse the traces of materiality and bodies in our relationship to artistic representation.

In this context, in Maso's "most unusual book," the white spaces surprise us, as they are not accustomed to fracture lines of prose, but they allow us to find what is "beyond" "within" the novel: white spaces reveal that they constitute, physically, the book that we read, even though we are used to taking the physical page for granted when we focus on the message of novels (*AVA* 70). Such an interest in what we have taken for granted in prose-writing relates to Maso's wish to explore "everything that's been kept out" of literature, "past and present," echoed in Ava's request "Don't leave anything out" (*Break* 191; *AVA* 262). The white space, while part of every printed material, has been "kept out" of literature in the form in which Maso uses it. As we will observe in chapter four and chapter five, Cha and Tomasula also explore what has been "kept out of literature" in their uses of textual materiality.

In Maso's work, the material of the page calls attention to the paradox at work in the relation between Ava's story and its absence. We accept the white spaces, as we realize that they *are* the material of the book, but at the same time, we tend to refuse their intrusion since they "resist 'inclusion'" in the representation of Ava and "resist identification or closure": they "represent much less than [they] self-present" (Didi-Huberman 268, 271). Because they point out their self-presentation, the white spaces threaten to disintegrate the story. This threat requires that we consider the medium the artist uses and its mode of representation. That is why Didi-Huberman concludes that the *pan* is a "not-yet [. . .] a 'quasi'-existence of the figure" (269). But this is where the *pan* and the white spaces differ: in *AVA,* the spaces between words are not pre-word materials, which would imply that they lack something.

A misconception of white space as pre-language often leads readers of Maso's "intricate and unusual production" to interpret them as a denunciation of the powerlessness of linguistic structures (*AVA* 139). The silence associated with the white spaces seems to materialize something missing because "silence does not have a grammatical form—we cannot diagram a moment of silence" (Berlin). That is why Monica Berlin claims that the white spaces represent "the healing of silence": "The textual spacing in *AVA*, as well as the character's own attraction toward quiet, implies that muting allows for empowerment of the self and that silence is more true than meaning produced in language." Berlin's insistence on the opposition between language and textual spacing implies that the white spaces are simply a void that directs us back to the lack of power of language. Karen Lee Osborne proposes a comparable interpretation of white spaces, for "The novel's silences evoke its hesitation, its syncopated distrust of words even as it limps toward them." This understanding of the novel relies on an opposition between the "expressive" words and the white spaces between them, which Osborne interprets as a lack of expressivity. Nicole Cooley compares the white space between lines to cuts between film sequences, a concept that leads her to focus on "the interstices where something appears to be missing," implying that "the reader must fill the interval of silence." While I do not disagree that Ava's fragmented thoughts can relate to cross-cutting montage in film, I do not concur with Cooley's, Berlin's, and Osborne's analyses of the white space as something "missing," but instead, as I shall argue in this chapter, see it as a figuration of the textual body.

Although the qualities of silence are difficult to grasp, Maso's exploration of white space should not be mistaken for the indication of a lack. Rather, as Berry points out, what is important is the presence of this seeming disappearance of the text on the page, which is not emptiness. According to Berry, the white spaces reveal the "autonomy, this material subsistence [that] threatens to make every page immaterial, as negligible as earth underfoot" (125). He suggests that the white spaces in *AVA* are not used primarily as the "spatial equivalent of a break in speech, a breath stop or syntactic division," as they are used in modern poetry (117). It is important to note that, while Maso's use of the white page is not comparable to line breaks in modern poetry, it shares affinities with poetic visual experiments, originally put forth by Stéphane Mallarmé in "Un coup de dés." Unlike Maso, Mallarmé uses not only the space of the page but also the arrangement of letters and typefaces to emulate the movement of the dice. However, the outcome of Mallarmé's spatial and visual manipulation comes close to the effect of Maso's white spaces. In both texts, the page is not merely an illustration of the text or the materialization of a syntactic pause. Instead, the reading of such pages relies on "a figural, visual, mode" that comes from "the effect of language arranged to make a form independent of the grammatical order of the words" (Drucker *The Visible* 59). As Drucker notes, "figuration belongs properly to the *presentational* rather than to the *representational*" (*The Visible* 59). This implies that, like in Mallarmé's work, Maso's white spaces do not represent "an already extant idea" but "bring something into being in its making" (*The Visible* 59).

Maso's exploration of "the *presentational*" and of "the *representational*" shares a common interest (the exploration of the page as a material object that has to be *seen*) with other postmodern books such as Federman's *Take It or Leave It* and David Markson's *Wittgenstein's Mistress,* where they foreground the character's speech, or materialize a battle between silence and speech (Berry 117–23). These novels *look like AVA* in their separation of prose by white space, but these white spaces are dependent upon the narrative: they express the character's and the narrator's voice. Even in novels, such as Percival Everett's *Walk Me to the Distance,* where line breaks do not resemble those in *AVA* but present a progressive appropriation of words by white pages, the white space is still symbolic of an extant idea. In Everett's work, at first, the chapters are very close together, with no page breaks between them. As characters evolve—David Larson adjusts to his new life after serving in the Vietnam War—the white separations between chapters become larger, and toward the end, the chapters are shorter. The book ends with four white pages that make the experience of reading comparable to "the becoming at home and of the western landscape, of adjusting to that wide open sense, of moving from the congestion of having just returned from Vietnam" (Everett, personal interview). Like in Federman's and Markson's work, Everett's page strikes us as *present,* but unlike Maso's novel, *Walk Me to the Distance* uses the page to express its linguistic content.

In *AVA,* we realize that the blank page is not an expression of linguistic codes, nor is it just the condition of writing. "The spaces between words. Between thoughts. The interval" are re-viewed so that they become part of the figural aspect of the text (*AVA* 171). Whiteness, in that sense, is a positive space, discernible from nothingness. As Gilbert-Rolfe indicates, while blankness used to be "a condition that [could] only point to a beginning or an end," "the late twentieth century has available to it the possibility of blankness as an activity, something happening now" (163). He adds that blankness is "neither the absence of expression nor a particular expression, but the possibility of expression in the sense of a presentation of the conditions of expression. This is one sense in which blankness is more easily described as an excess than as an absence in the contemporary situation"

(167). Gilbert-Rolfe's and Berry's studies remind us that the white spaces in *AVA* are not merely places meant for words to whisk across and down the page, nor are they expressing or representing something. They call attention to the possibility of any writing, so that blankness "has become signally characteristic of the surface of all the signs which exclude it with recognizability and narrative, that is, which seek to subsume it within form and formality, shape and protocol, urge and economy" (Gilbert-Rolfe 175). Here, Gilbert-Rolfe suggests that the twentieth century's use of blankness in visual arts has made visible the white surface that was taken for granted before.

Susan Howe's writing on the question of white space and materiality in painting and literature is useful here. Inspired by minimalist painters, Howe writes about Ad Reinhart's black paintings, Malevich's white on white works, and Rodchenko's black on black paintings in relation to Ian Hamilton Finlay's concrete poems. For her, the unsaid page and the unpainted canvas are as expressive as words and paint; the painter's and writer's task is to allow whiteness to become part of art. The artists she studies reveal that "to search for infinity inside simplicity will be to find simplicity alive with messages" ("The End of Art" 7). Howe associates the simplicity of minimalist paintings and poems with images of "infinity": the sea, "the silent voice," the nothingness that precedes art ("The End of Art" 8). Maso's use of white space differs from Howe's interest in nothingness, as in *AVA* the white space does not express a silence or a void in opposition to the expressive words on it. However, Howe's consideration of the physical immediacy of the white expanses in poetry and painting as primordial to our relationship to art is useful to reading Maso's work: Howe explains that our considerations of the meaningful and meaningless are often erroneous. In *The Birth-Mark*, she focuses on Thomas Shepard's manuscripts and their eighty-six blank pages followed by "another narrative by the same author" written upside down from the other text (58). Editors have included parts of the second text as "notes," but excluded the blank pages from the book, which Howe considers a misreading of the white space of Shepard's work. Howe also indicates that Dickinson's irregular spacing, also omitted from Dickinson's published work, is part of the meaning of her text. As Walter Benn Michaels points out, Howe's commitment to the white page asks important questions about reading and writing: "What do you have to think reading is to think that when you run your eyes over blank pages you are reading them? Or what do you have to think a text is to think that pages without writing are part of it?" (1). If we agree with Howe's claim that the white expanses of a text are to be *read,* then whiteness is intrinsic to *any* reading process, and Maso's text makes this realization part of the experience of her text. In *AVA,* the white spaces invite us to become aware of the surface of the text, that which made it possible:

> A page is not a surface onto which a preexisting entity, such as a novel, has been laid, nor is it an agglomeration of particles. A page is the presence of a novel before my presence to it, after its presence to me. This very autonomy, this material subsistence, threatens to make every page immaterial, as negligible as earth underfoot. Maso makes hers matter again, uncovers her page's presence, by making its space our means, almost our only means, of telling Ava's life from an agglomeration. (Berry 125)

Like Berry, I insist that the white spaces call attention to the materiality of the novel, and to some extent, comment metafictionally on the nature of writing. Building on his demonstration, I wish to clarify the implications of our recognition of the "material subsistence" of the page. As I hope to show, our acknowledgment of textual materiality calls for a physical engagement with writing, which triggers a reexamination of the importance of the body in reading methodologies. In *AVA*, Maso's use of textual materiality calls for an engagement of the erotic body. This engagement is constitutive of a relationship with the text that does not exist merely as an oppositional discourse. While *AVA* evidently proposes a mode of writing and reading that subverts patriarchal models, framing the novel strictly in a resistant aesthetic would leave aside the positive creation that comes out of *AVA*'s transformative reading practices.

Indeed, this transformation comes from the breathed white expansions escaping from Ava's body. As Maso explains, in writing *AVA,* "this is what literature became for me: music, love, and the body. I cannot keep the body out of my writing; it enters language, transforms the page, imposes its own intelligence. If I have succeeded at all you will hear me breathing" (*Break* 70). In characterizing her text as a trembling and shuddering one and in exposing its breathing qualities, Maso places our reading in a bodily and erotic realm. This body "trembles and shudders" through the fragments of Ava's life, making *AVA* "a living text. One that trembles and shudders. One that yearns. It is filled with ephemeral thoughts, incomplete gestures, revisions, recurrences, and repetitions—precious, disappearing things" (*Break* 64). The white spaces that bring to life the trembling body are akin to the intermittence of the erotic body that flashes skin, revealing the "the staging of an appearance-as-disappearance" (*Pleasure* 10). Our relationship to this "appearance-as-disappearance" does not rely on a striptease-like relationship to the body/text: we are not longing for the naked body, nor are we longing for a total understanding of the thoughts that Ava may be trying to express. Instead, as the text unveils itself as an erotic body, we long for the physical page in our hands.

Barthes compares the unveiling of body and text because both become erotic, not in their nudity or graphic representation of sexuality, but in the cracks, the showing of the skin between clothes, the in-between-ness, and the contrasting texture of the different surfaces: "Is not the most erotic position of a body *where the garment gapes?* [. . .] [I]t is intermittence [. . .] which is erotic: the intermittence of skin flashing between two articles of clothing [. . .]; it is this flash itself which seduces" (*Pleasure* 9–10). The white spaces compare to this erotic body because, in itself, the page is not an object of desire, just as the naked body is not an object of desire. Yet, when the body goes beyond its daily functions, it acquires an erotic force. The veiling of the body/text triggers perversity because it invites us to focus on its materiality instead of its functions. In *AVA,* the white spaces become ecstatic because they evade their traditional role: the page, the textual support, gains significance. It is not a mere substance that carries a linguistic message. Instead, it becomes meaningful because the way Maso conveys and organizes information is part of the message of the novel. Maso uses white space to question the role and power of the page as it functions in relation to representation, while at the same time frustrating any attempt to categorize such representation in conventional ways. Thus, she enables us to recognize that texts are more than successions of words and spaces. Like Ava, we "fee[l] form—finally. / A more spacious form. After all this time. / Breathe" (212). Our reading becomes a progressive unveiling of the white pages, discovering "the seduction that is, that has always been language" (227). Because the seduction of the page forces us to go beyond traditional representational techniques and to engage with the material of the book, *AVA* demands that we adopt embodied reading techniques. Such techniques allow us to come closer to the materiality of the text and discover what is not "visible" to us in other texts: the page.

Hence, while at first it appears that we long for the unified and straightforward story of Ava and interpret the white space as a distraction from our goal, we learn to reexamine the role of the materiality of texts as we keep reading, or "the interaction of physical characteristics [of a text] with its signifying strategies" (Hayles 103). In recognizing what we had suppressed from our reading—that is, the active role of the physical characteristics in the signification of a text—we realize that our desire was in fact for the veiling and unveiling of the white page. In ordinary texts, the page is only desirable as a site of something else, but in reading *AVA,* we acknowledge the material support of meaning as central to our reading experience. However, the erotic site of the page does not negate the significance of language. The interdependence of language and silence makes us aware of the page as a medium, hence of the words as medium of this page as well. Maso discloses what has been repressed in novels through her veiling and unveiling of the page and language, the alternation of which creates reading methods akin to sexual foreplay. Because she emphasizes the process and constructed-ness of the medium she is using, she refashions it, while inviting the reader to engage erotically with it.

This engagement with the text enables healing and separation, to use Cixous's word. Indeed, in the novel, Ava repeatedly recalls Cixous's wish "to create a language that heals as much as it separates" (52). Cixous calls for an embrace of both poles in *écriture féminine*. For her, women should attain this paradoxical locus in bodily writing. *AVA* is an example of such bodily writing, not only through its treatment of language but through its use of white space. As Silbergleid suggests, this paradoxical mode of writing relies on Maso's use of white spaces: "While Maso's textual silences appear to condone separation—her fragments literally broken by white space on the page—these textual blanks also enable Maso to move toward a language that heals in *AVA*, a language that brings together and repairs" (18). Thus, the white spaces stand in-between and express the goal Cixous gives to language. What Maso reveals is that such healing and separateness lie not only in language, as Cixous implies, but also in the material structures of literature that have become unconscious to us. For her, such unconscious structures also rely on the repression of the body from texts. In that sense, she remains indebted to Cixous, as both writers believe that women's empowerment lies in the exploration of writing, and more precisely in the interrelation of such writing with the body. However, Maso adds the misrecognized power of the materiality of books to Cixous's emphasis on language's ability to affect women's representations of their body.

This emphasis on materiality is important because it clarifies the writing and reading method Cixous calls for in "The Laugh of the Medusa" and "Sorties," where her description of a bodily text remains abstract. In shifting the focus from a linguistic exploration to a linguistic *and* material exploration, Maso allows us to experience a bodily text. Such a text requires that we engage in the textual medium, which allows us to practice the feminist bodily methodology Cixous and Maso rely on. In that sense, the attention Maso gives to textual materiality requires new reading and interpretive methods that recognize texts as more than sequences of words and spaces, and readers as physical and intellectual entities. In going beyond

Cixous's claim about *écriture féminine,* Maso proves that it is necessary to reconceptualize our interpretive tools to take the role of the body in relation to materiality more fully into account. As we shall see in the next chapters, visual materiality calls for a haptic relationship with texts, thereby enabling an erotic fusion of reader and text. This tactile approach to reading is a pleasurable, affirmative production that exists not merely as a subversion of traditional reading methods—though it is also that—but as a powerful positive production of its own.

Some will not know age. no age. Time stops. Time will
stop for some. For them especially. Eternal time. No age.
No deterioration. Time fixes for some. In their view
Their image, the memory, them. On their countenance
the hallowed beauty that is past evidence
captured
Standing before hallowed beauty. The only Beauty, because of the
, only because
loss, the absence, the object presents the loss, the
exposes
missing that left to the imaginary. Evokes not the
Their countenance evokes not the beauty, restoring decay
the hallowed beauty from the
the inevitable the dy-ing.
not death, but

Standing before hallowed beauty. The beauty, that it only because
Standing face to face with the memory memory of It misses. it's
missing. still. what of time. do not move. remains there.
Misses nothing. Time, that is. all else. all things else.
all of things other. Subject to time. Must answer to time.
Time dictates all else, except some. It misses. all installed in time,

chapter four

Erotics and Corporeality in Theresa Hak Kyung Cha's *DICTEE*

This excerpt from Cha's draft figures at the end of *DICTEE*'s chapter "CLIO HISTORY," which documents the Japanese invasion of Korea and the actions of the revolutionary Yu Guan Soon. Soon's struggles correlate with other female figures' physical, psychological, and emotional trials recorded through painful linguistic processes: women's uttering, telling, and narrating are dissected and tormented in the novel (see figure 11). In the above excerpt, the physical changes, deletions, and corrections are expressions of the "decapitated forms. Worn. Marred, recording a past, of previous forms" (38), of the torturing linguistic practices ("Swallows with last efforts last wills against the pain that wishes it to speak" 3), and of Soon's physical torture. The chapter itself documents some of these struggles: we find information on Japan and the Japanese occupation (28–30); diary entries from Hyung Soon Huo, Cha's mother (31); the article "SUP-PRESSION OF FOREIGN CRITICISM" (31); the "PETITION FROM THE KOREANS OF HAWAII TO PRESIDENT ROOSEVELT" (34); a photograph of Japanese soldiers and Korean nationalists (39); and the above draft of page 37 (40–41). This collage of information points to the gaps in history and to the contradictions that undermine official accounts of the colonization of Korea. In Cha's draft, deletions, additions, and alterations further stress the artificiality of historical writing, which, like fiction, is rearranged and manipulated. The fact that a draft appears with "official" historical accounts raises questions about sources, authenticity, and history. All the documents listed above may be the author's fabrication; all writings, including historical reports, are fictional.

Cha's presentation of her unfinished work also underlines the material structures that are part of writing, bringing her text close to previous fictions that have made the peripheral materials of writing and publishing part of the artistic realm. Gilbert Sorrentino's *Mulligan Stew* is an example of metafictional uses of peripheral texts: the novel opens on several presses' rejection letters of the novel that we are about to read. Like Sorrentino, Cha stresses the crafted quality of her work and calls attention to its fiction-ness when reproducing her draft in *DICTEE*. But Cha's handwritten page also calls attention to the physicality of language, which correlates with her use of puns, bilingual expressions, and poetic explorations. Her linguistic experiments obtrude a transparent relationship to language, inviting us to *look* at the text. The handwritten pages of *DICTEE* stress this nontransparent approach to language and textual materiality, as words have a physical presence that we tend to overlook when they are typed. As Drucker notes in her visually experimental essay, "Visual/ Verbal: Symposium Response," "HANDWRITING" "TACKL[ES] THE TASK OF MAKING ITSELF," "ESCAP[ING] ITS OWN CONTAINMENT" (143), so that "THE HOT FORM OF **LETTERS** ON A PAGE" (142) fosters "WRESTLING, EMBRACING, **STRUGGLING,** WITH THE EXPRESSIVE FORM IN APPREHENSION" (*Figuring* 142). The physical presence of the handwritten page invites "THE EYE, DELIGHTED, [to] RETUR[N] THE ABSENT, ELUSIVE **PROPERTIES** OF SUGGESTION TO THE BODY OF THE TEXT, **ENJOYING** BOTH PLEASURE AND FRUSTRATION" (*Figuring* 142–43). The eye's concentration on the material substance of the text brings the handwritten page to signify not only through its content but also through its bodily presence.

In Cha's work, the use of the handwritten page also calls attention to the white space underneath it, which, under the black scribbles, is more apparent. In *DICTEE*, the white page does not function as a breathed body, as it does in *AVA*, but Cha, like Maso, stresses the importance of the materiality of the white expanses on pages 40 and 41. The spots of white space and the untidy black handwriting serve Cha's exploration of the themes of whiteness and blackness, of the act of erasing or blacking out narratives, and of racial discrimination. In fact, *DICTEE* figures white pages separating each section and interrupting the text, on page 107, for example. These pages present another mode of exploration of the struggles of expression in the context of social censure, patriarchal domination, and colonial violence. *DICTEE*'s white pages are enactments of the oppressiveness of social powers, that "void" and "silence" protagonists (73). Yet, in materializing a possibility, these "unwritten" pages also propose another mode of expression in "the present form to face to face reveals the missing, the absent. Would-be-said remnant, memory. But the remnant is the whole" (38). White pages explore a "form" that, much like in *AVA*, reminds us of what we fail to consider, yet is always there as a "whole"—the page. Cha's play with the material presence of the page leads to a reflection on the relationship between text and gender and on their influence on identity, race, and ethnicity. The complex relationship between these different aspects of Cha's project have made it difficult to frame *DICTEE* within one literary approach, which is why interpretations of Cha's work often engage in a reevaluation of the analytical tools available to approach texts such as *DICTEE*.

Because Cha is a Korean American writer whose parents settled in California, readers expect that, like the works of many Asian American novelists of the 1980s, *DICTEE* deals with the formation of the author's Korean yet American identity. As a result, critics often emphasize the surprise and challenge they experienced during their first encounter with *DICTEE*. Cha's research on a nontransparent access to language astonishes them, as does her exploration of a fragmented identity through the fragmented text.[1] Readers note that Cha's work does not, like other Asian texts of the 1980s, construct a clear Korean subjectivity.[2] In addition, *DICTEE* not only challenges the traditional autobiographical ethnic mode, it also disturbs the reader's expectations by breaking down boundaries between genres and playing with them. For example, *DICTEE* opens with a list of nine Greek muses, each

---

1. Laura Hyun Yi Kang's reading response, for example, is particularly compelling: "It angered me that the text was not always accessible, that it seemed to speak to a highly literate, theoretically sophisticated audience that I did not identify with. Most of all, Cha herself remained elusive [. . .]. I believed that I, as a Korean/American woman, should be able to immediately understand and identify with the work of another Korean/American woman, and since that mirroring/attraction did not happen, either must there be something 'wrong' with me or her" (76). Elaine Kim writes, "The first time I glanced at *Dictée*, I was put off by the book. I thought that Theresa Cha was talking not to me but rather to someone so remote from myself that I could not recognize 'him.' The most I could hope for, I thought, was to be permitted to stand beside her while she addressed 'him'" (3).

2. See the works of Amy Tan, Cynthia Kadohata, David Henry Hwang, Wendy Law-Yone, Hi-saye Yamamoto, Hualing Nieh, and Evelyn Lau.

attributed to a section of the book (Clio, Calliope, Urania, Melpomene, Erato, Elitere, Thalia, Terpsichore, and Polymnia), and readers seem invited to use classic literature to explore Cha's narrative. However, this interpretive tool is questioned, since Cha changes Euterpe's name to Elitere, complicating the seemingly simple connection between each section and a muse.[3] Furthermore, Cha relies on a well-known structure of the Christian Trinity, but replaces it with Joan of Arc, the Korean revolutionary Yu Guan Soon, and Sainte Thérèse. Here again, she shocks her reader by distorting the familiar (Oh 7). Nevertheless, such distortion does not construct a clear Korean American identity.

The lack of guidance on how to relate the formal experiments with print, page, orthography, and syntax and the Korean specificities of the novel has led critics to follow two paths: the first investigates Cha's linguistic innovation in relation to post-structural theory, and explores Cha's rendering of difference and hybridity through language. That is, these critics, especially Juliana Spahr, Kristen Twelbeck, and Eun Kyung Min, interpret the difficulty of the text as a mode of expression that enables Cha's voice to transcend a strictly Korean context.[4] The second interprets Cha's work as a redefinition of the Asian American identity using postcolonial theory. In other words, the difficulty of Cha's text is a means of exploring a new Korean voice.[5] Both interpretations of Cha's writing disclose the limitations in our interpretive discourses, revealing the shortcomings of cultural studies'

---

3. For a discussion of the subversiveness of the re-naming of the muse, see Shelley Sunn Wong's, Kristina Chew's, and Anita Choe's works on *DICTEE*.

4. For Spahr, *DICTEE's* linguistic and syntactic challenges offer a practical form of decolonization: the lack of control the reader might have over the text (through the deformation of literary conventions, shifts of languages and media, and syntactic manipulations) prevents the reader from colonizing it. For Min, the play on citations in *DICTEE* deprives it of referential value, and fosters a reflection on the lack of knowledge and control. In Spahr's and Min's arguments, Cha's experiments with the (de)colonization of the subject and the text go beyond Korean historical and material specificities.

5. This second trend of criticism condemns post-structural readings that essentialize Cha's message by transforming it into a universal expression of female writing and erasing Korean history. As Shelley Sunn Wong explains, in "invoking concepts of 'hybridity,' 'alterity,' and 'difference,'" these readings are "often unable to bind these concepts to the specific and material historical conditions out of which Cha attempted to speak the difference of the Korean American immigrant woman" (65). The collection of essays *Writing Self, Writing Nation*, edited by Elaine Kim and Norma Alarcón, also emphasizes the historical and social particularities of *DICTEE*, opposing the early interpretations of the novel that came from postmodern and avant-garde critics. These essays highlight Cha's opposition to the domination by Western culture in her disruption of dictation (when a student unquestioningly writes what he or she hears in another language), while also stressing that Cha presents images of colonial resistance through the revolutionary figures Yu Guan Soon, Isang Yun, and her own mother.

exploration of ethnic authenticity and of the abstraction of the post-structural reading of Cha's postmodern aesthetics. As Warren Tswun-Hwa Liu points out, *DICTEE* asks us to consider how a text can express a Korean experience while showing the limits of such a mode of expression insofar as it relies on nationalism. The critical writing on *DICTEE* performs exactly what Cha problematizes: assimilation and absorption.

In an attempt to do justice to Cha's linguistic experiments while rooting them in a Korean immigrant context, most recent readings of *DICTEE* follow a dialectical pattern, first acknowledging that Cha's mode of writing is not realistic and does not depict an authentic Korean identity, then presenting her linguistic experiments as expressions of a different and hybrid identity.[6] This new identity is then re-framed as a new representation of Asian American identity. Conversely, this last move is contrary to Cha's project. since her exploration of multiplicity, hybridity, and "non-identity" does not return to a rooting place (Lowe 56). This framing of Cha's work within a Korean context is troublesome, as it speaks not "*with*" but *for DICTEE*" (Twelbeck 227). Thus, analyses that consider Cha's linguistic experiments as a *source* of knowledge misread her text: she challenges this very concept in her exploration of the emotional and geopolitical difficulties of transnational contexts. Cha does not recognize Korea as the only principle of identification but instead reveals the complexities of the adoption of different languages and cultural behaviors. Indeed, Cha defies "politics of inclusion and exclusion [. . .] where arbitrarily fixed categories of identity in the form of identity politics can police cultural expressions and practices" (Lionnet and Shih 10). In *DICTEE*, such categories are negotiated through female figures' struggle in reclaiming their cultural identity during and/or after colonization and exile. Yet, Cha also stresses the characters' transnational status and the dangers of recapturing a "pure" Korean identity, as she challenges unified and stable cultural productions. Thus, she emphasizes the hybrid and relational position of her characters and of her linguistic expressions.[7]

I do not wish to negate the importance of the Korean context of Cha's work, or her political response to western and patriarchal models, but I want to overcome the limitations of reading that "take the sensory experiences of the work of art for granted, and procee[d] from there" (Sontag 13).

---

6. See Sue-Im Lee's or Helena Grice's works, for example.

7. Spahr, Twelbeck, and Min focus on such expressions and emphasize Cha's formal and thematic disruptions in relation to postmodern writers, such as Robert Duncan and Charles Olson. In fact, both Cha's postgraduate work with Christian Metz, Raymond Bellour, and Thierry Kuntzel in Paris in 1976 and her performances were influenced by the psychoanalytic aspects of French film theory and share affinities with formally innovative works of the 1970s and post-structural theories.

Analyses of *DICTEE* tend to focus more on her responses to traditional narrative and ideologies than on her pleasurable production. I propose to focus instead on *"The labor of tongues. [. . .] The labor of voices."* to demonstrate that openness and fluidity allow a fusion of subject and object, which invites an erotic relationship with language (161).[8] In Cha's text, the connection between writing and the body is clear from the beginning of the book where Cha quotes Sappho: "May I write words more naked than flesh, / stronger than bone, more resilient than / sinew, sensitive than nerve," framing her work within a tradition of texts that link the flesh and words.[9] In Cha's text, the bodily and the textual are not strictly separated:

> Secrete saliva the words
> Saliva secrete the words
> Secretion of words flow liquid form
> Salivate the words.

FIGURE 12. Theresa Hak Kyung Cha. *DICTEE* p. 130 (c) 2001 The Regents of the University of California. The University of California Press.

In this passage, Cha reinforces the bodily aspect of linguistic expression (see figure 12). The saliva, the "abject" that the mind needs to control in models of thoughts inspired by Descartes, participates in words' formation. Conversely, Cha's varying of sentence organization allows the reader to pay attention to the materiality of language, breaking down boundaries between linguistic immateriality and bodily materiality because, for her, *"Thought [is] as visible as words as act"* (*DICTEE* 17).

---

8. Iulia Csorvasi also proposes an analysis of Cha's new syntax, which "transfer[s] the fluid character of the woman subject into language" (53). My own approach differs from hers in that she focuses strictly on thematic fluidity through an exploration of the multiplicity inherent in Korean feminine identity, the multi-vocal characters, the crossing of geographical boundaries, and the blurring of genres. I wish to acknowledge the linguistic openness of the text, which, on a structural *and* formal level, produces an erotic language at the origin of Cha's feminist project.

9. *DICTEE's* fragmentariness emulates Sappho's poetic fragments, and Cha's female speakers echo Sappho's feminine poetic voice. The sensuousness of Cha's language and her concentration on corporeality also evoke Sappho's focus on passion, love, and Eros. However, according to Chew, "An examination of the manuscript evidence of Sappho reveals that no such lines exist in the poet's extant writing, indicating that Cha has made them up" (218). Here, Cha invokes the authority of the woman poet and the Western literary tradition associated with her, but modifies these canonical texts in her re-writing of history and women's roles.

Cha writes, "Unfathomable the words, the terminology: enemy, atroci-ties, conquest, betrayal, invasion, destruction [. . . .] Not physical enough. Not to the very flesh and bone, to the core, to the mark, to the point where it is necessary to intervene" (32). Her emphasis on the physical nature of language meets Cixous's aspirations in her exploration of *écriture féminine* and the Third Body, where the relationship between the body and the text is ever-changing (32).[10] In her essay "Sorties," Cixous explains that a woman is "in the suspense, in what will soon be, always differed" (67). Cixous implies two things. First, the feminine cannot be represented, but it can be translated into the deferment activity of language. Second, this deferment activity relies on language's capacity for play. This playful enjoyment of lan-guage's materiality participates in Cha's positive political production. She plays with the term "diseuse," which inserts a pun in the text since it is close to "disease" and "disuse." Cha further plays with these words in the Elitere section (see figure 13):

> Dead words. Dead tongue. From disuse. Buried in
> Time's memory. Unemployed. Unspoken. History.
> Past. Let the one who is diseuse, one who is mother
> who waits nine days and nine nights be found.
> Restore memory. Let the one who is diseuse, one
> who is daughter restore spring with her each ap-
> pearance from beneath the earth.
> The ink spills thickest before it runs dry before it
> stops writing at all.

FIGURE 13. Theresa Hak Kyung Cha. *DICTEE* p. 133 (c) 2001 The Regents of the University of California. The University of California Press.

Cha's insistence on feminine figures (the mother, the daughter, the diseuse) in relation to writing evokes Cixous's statement on *écriture féminine*. As Stella Oh points out, "Cha assumes the role of the *diseuse* who will utter the memory of the suppressed and redress the (dis)use and (mis)use of women" (16). The play on words with "*disuse*" alludes to the misusage of words that cannot "*restore memory*" as opposed to the mother and daughter who have this ability. Like Cixous, Cha denounces the oppressiveness of patriarchal language, a language that has written and spoken women's history. Conse-

---

10. Deborah Mix, Kun Jong Lee, and Karina Eileraas also mention that Cha's attention to the body recalls Hélène Cixous's invitation for women to "write [themselves]" ("Laugh" 875).

quently, in their works, the pun reveals linguistic and historical patriarchal biases. To eradicate such biases, Cixous proposes that women find signifying processes that transcend patriarchal models. While the subversive qualities of Cixous's and Cha's works have been emphasized in past readings, the positive production that is indistinguishable from the subversiveness of their work remains unexamined. This positive production derives from in-between sensations and realities, or what Cixous calls the Third Body, "that which is projected outside of me and covers over me, this body foreign to my body that rises from my body and shrouds it" (*Third* 34). At the beginning of the "DISEUSE" section, Cha explores voices akin to the interior and exterior realities of the Third Body (see figure 14):

DISEUSE

She mimicks the speaking. That might resemble speech. (Anything at all.) Bared noise, groan, bits torn from words. Since she hesitates to measure the accuracy, she resorts to mimicking gestures with the mouth. The entire lower lip would lift upwards then sink back to its original place. She would then gather both lips and protrude them in a pout taking in the breath that might utter some thing. (One thing. Just one.) But the breath falls away. With a slight tilting of her head backwards, she would gather the strength in her shoulders and remain in this position.

FIGURE 14. Theresa Hak Kyung Cha. *DICTEE* p. 3 (c) 2001 The Regents of the University of California. The University of California Press.

Numerous critics have made claims about the source of the voice in this excerpt, attributing "she" to Cha or the "diseuse" figure.[11] Like Liu, I believe that the ambiguity of this passage is what is important, not its possible clarification. Therefore, instead of attributing a stable source to the voice of the passage, I conceive of the unidentifiable voice in relation to the Third Body. In addition to ambiguity in the attribution of "she," the parenthetical interruptions are also intriguing since they comment on the activity that is happening in the passage, "ruptur[ing] the narrative of the speaker by doubling the speaker's position as at once a third-person observer and a first-person

---

11. Kim associates the "diseuse" with the Korean entertainer (kisaneng) (14). Wong compares the "diseuse" to a Greek figure. For Liu, the "diseuse" is "'an embodied form of translator,' through which the subject speaks and imagines herself" (52).

actor" (Liu 55). This in-between entity evokes Cixous's Third Body, a body that is in-between (the speaker and the reader, the observer and the actor), and without a clear origin. On the other hand, the lack of clear separation between the narrator, "she," and the parenthetical "other" sets up the erotic mechanism from the start of the novel: the lack of clear boundaries between subject and object allows the dissolution of the subject that is at the origin of the erotic experience.

While in this passage Cha emphasizes the role of language in this erotic process, in the rest of the novel she also highlights the position of language as a means of communication that connects or excludes people; it is *between* them.[12] This in-between-ness relies on Cha's use of different languages that she does not always translate, the foreignness of her English text, and the absence of captions to her visual texts. These techniques invite the reader to associate freely the different pieces of the hybrid novel. When reading, the reader shifts to and from controlling positions, in regard to the portions of a language he or she might know and when connecting different parts that make sense together, to a lack of control; when the text does not *mean*, in the traditional sense; when encountering a foreign language; or when feeling that Cha is making an intertextual reference to a text that one does not know. These alternations between controlling and surrendering positions parallel erotic processes, while calling attention to the linguistic material of the text. By stressing the materiality of her work and its open qualities, Cha allows the viewer to give up his or her own sense of separateness from the text. Such fusion with the text imitates an erotic embodied gesture, which reshapes our reading methodologies. In that sense, much like Maso, Cha invites us to reconsider textual materiality as inherent in feminist practices when sensually engaging us in visual and linguistic materials.

Thus, *DICTEE* forces the reader to adopt new reading techniques that do not rely on literal meaning because the "'stuttering,' grammatically 'incorrect,' and linguistically hybrid" language in the novel suspends the limits of "subjectivity," which expands "through a kind of 'contact' with [one's] 'own' Other" (Twelbeck 232, 235). Twelbeck shows that the stuttering voice, the musical rhythms, and "broken language" "indicat[e] that we

---

12. *DICTEE's* in-between-ness has been emphasized in a number of ways—the translation mode situates the text between two languages (Lowe, Berila, Chang "Word"); films and letters are in-between figures (between sender and receiver, and viewer and artist) (Park); *DICTEE* is between epic and lyric modes (Wong); Cha's work is between fiction and history (Mix); the female exiled woman is in-between (Csorvasi); *DICTEE* branches into oral and written realms (Min); *DICTEE* is between organicism and technology (Chang "Word"). Hence, it would be redundant to explore every aspect of the novel's in-between-ness. I will thus focus strictly on in-between-ness in relation to the erotics of the text.

[. . .] dispose of a capacity to experience [*DICTEE*'s] polyvocal 'slipperiness' (Kang 1995: 76) and disruptive structure as meaningful and enjoyable" (237). Cha's use of language thus asks that we yield to the sensuousness of the words, an experience close to the experience of the Semiotic, as defined in chapters one and two: here, plays on sounds and rhythms eliminate the distance between reader and text. In *DICTEE*, the inassimilable excess of meaning of the impenetrable text produces a different kind of reading, one that goes beyond literal meaning and asks that we take pleasure in the linguistic material of the novel (see figure 15):

> It had been snowing. During the while.
> Interval. Recess. Pause.
> It snowed. The name. The term. The noun.
> It had snowed. The verb. The predicate. The act of.
> Fell.
> Luminescent substance more so in black night.
> Inwardly luscent. More. So much so that its entry
> closes the eyes
> Interim. Briefly.
> In the enclosed darkness memory is fugitive.
> Of white. Mist offers to snow self
> In the weightless slow all the time it takes long
> ages precedes time pronounces it alone on its own
> while. In the whiteness
> no distinction her body invariable no dissonance
> synonymous her body all the time de composes
> eclipses to be come yours.

FIGURE 15. Theresa Hak Kyung Cha. *DICTEE* p. 118 (c) 2001 The Regents of the University of California. The University of California Press.

Cha plays with idioms, allowing a disruption of our automatisms: "for a while" becomes "during the while," forcing the English language to bear the marks of her foreignness. As "for" and "during" translate the same idea here, the difference between them is hard to pinpoint for a speaker who does not control the idiomatic usages of English. The linguistic variation "It snowed. The name. The term. The noun. / It had snowed. The verb. The predicate. The act of.", echoing the rigor and logic of grammar books, compels the reader to step away from the message of the passage and think in terms of grammatical issues, correctness, and rules. The shift from "it snowed" to "it had snowed" emphasizes semantically the nuances a grammatical change can make. The text is both a grammar lesson and a defamiliarization; it is a destruction of the very grammatical bearings it alludes to.

The thematic involvement of in-between moments, roles, and places echoes the in-between-ness of language: "Interval. Recess. Pause." and "Interim." express something in-between. The in-between-ness penetrates the different themes of the passage—snow and identity—allowing them to become permeable: "Mist offers to snow self." Finally, Cha's use of "de composes" reminds us that "decompose" contains its own antonym, "compose." In her sentence, this allows the body both to decay and to create. In the end, there is "no distinction," but this does not mean that everything equates anything. In using the word "synonymous," Cha reminds us (and we have an example of this in her use of "during") that words can express the same idea but still be different. This play on sameness and difference, which allows Cha to explore an "in-between" pleasurable language, takes place in her visual experiments as well.

The text shown in figure 15 faces a photograph of Renée Falconetti in Carl Dreyer's silent film *La Passion de Jeanne d'Arc* (1928), revealing Cha's interest in the relationship between the visual and written media. Cha explains, "My video, film, and performance work . . . are explorations of the language structures inherent in written and spoken material, photographic, and filmic images—the creation of new relationships and meanings in the simultaneity of these forms" (Cha qtd. in Lewallen 9). The simultaneity of these forms engages comparable disruptions in two different media: Cha's untraditional use of English and other languages makes the reader lose control over the progression of the narration. Similarly, her insertion of photos destabilizes the reader because the photograph representing Joan of Arc, like an unknown foreign language, is inaccessible to the reader if he or she is not familiar with the silent film.

Cha's use of obscure photographs can also be found in earlier attempts to combine visual and linguistic experiments. Ishmael Reed's *Mumbo Jumbo*, for example, includes photographs alongside citations, drawings, footnotes, and bibliographies on African American history to undermine cultural documentation. Like *DICTEE*, *Mumbo Jumbo* leaves some photographs uncaptioned or partially cited in order to highlight the gaps in Western culture's historical traditions. At times, Reed's selection of images illustrates the narrative, but not always. Thus, these images do not merely substantiate the narrative but interrupt its flow to undermine its stability. Similarly, *DICTEE* provokes doubts about the roles and goals of "History" and the stability of any texts. In Cha's work, the connections between images and written text are even looser than in Reed's: instead of rooting pictures in specific contexts, she prefers to leave them unspecified, so that they comment not on definite themes or times, but rather on their modes of representation, as her use of the photograph of Joan of Arc and the "ERATO LOVE POETRY" section illustrates (see figure 16):[13]

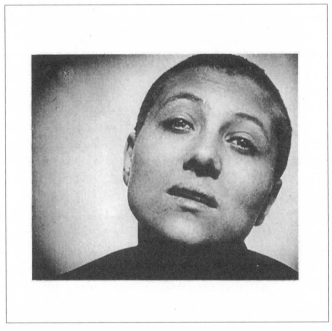

FIGURE 16. Theresa Hak Kyung Cha. *DICTEE* p. 119 (c) 2001 The Regents of the University of California. The University of California Press.

Cha chooses a close-up of Joan of Arc before she rejects the chance to confess, a refusal that leads to her death. The proximity of the camera in the film parallels the closeness of the narrator "Near front. Close to the screen" in the "ERATO LOVE POETRY" section, where a woman walks toward the screen in a theatre (94). It also mirrors "Extreme Close Up shot of her face" when the film is shown in the theatre, which this section depicts (96). Through the physical walk of the character, through her description of the close-up in the film, and through the choice of a still that shows the pigments and cracks of Dryer's film, Cha invites us to come close to the medium of her own text: "Then you, as a viewer and guest, enter the house. It is you

13. For a detailed discussion of Dryer's film and *DICTEE*, see Gordon Hadfield's *Sounding Time: Temporality, Typography, and Technology in Twentieth-Century American Poetry*.

who are entering to see her" (98). The "you" is ambiguous in this excerpt, as "you" can refer to a collective and plural person and to a singular "you" directed to someone. In this passage, "you" is probably a singular "you," used as an equivalent of "one," or the auto-referential "you" of the narrator addressing herself. However, it is possible to interpret these sentences as an invitation to the reader as well. In this case, the use of "you" is not unlike the metafictional gestures displayed in fictions of the sixties and seventies, such as Barth's declaration "Talking soberly of unimportant or irrelevant matters and listening consciously to the sound of your own voice are useful habits for maintaining control in this difficult interval" (72) or "You couldn't hear it without laughing yourself, no matter how you felt" (79) in *Lost in the Funhouse*. Cha's use of "you" resembles Barth's, as her metafictional intrusion breaks the illusion of the fictional world and draws the reader into the text. Yet, her metafictional disillusionment also reveals that there is no clear boundary between the art medium and the subject. In insisting on the closeness of the reader to the artistic material, Cha's aims are close to those of Maso, as both writers reveal that playing with the materials of books allows us to reconsider our reading and interpretive practices in a pleasurable fusion with the text.

Cha also explores materiality differently from Maso, as she uses images to configure another way to document women's lives and writing. Cha's emphasis on the visual medium correlates with her film background. Her work at the Centre d'Etudes Américaines du Cinéma à Paris in 1976 and her productions as a filmmaker, performance artist, and installation artist from 1977 to 1980 led her to reflect on representational issues.[14] In 1980 she edited *Apparatus: Cinematographic Apparatus. Selected Writings*, which, as Gordon Hadfield reminds us, dwells on the "cinematic apparatus, the malfunction, and the erasure of malfunction" (139). In *DICTEE* Cha draws attention to the imperfection of the pictorial medium by using the shot from Dryer's movie, as well as the overexposed picture of Yu Guan Soon (24), the deteriorated and torn photo of Hyung Soon Huo (59), and the blurry photograph of the Korean crowd (122). Hence, just as she questions the rules of language and its ability to communicate, Cha emphasizes the "corrosion of the film, in 'what misses,'" which renders the photography partially visible (Hadfield 141). In doing so, she comments on the ways in which each mode of representation frames and signifies its object and the ways in which these frames can be challenged. While I will expand on such representational strategies in chapter five, where I will deal with Tomasula's visual methods,

---

14. Cha's films and art installations are available at the Berkeley Art Museum.

I wish to clarify here the erotics of the in-between positioning of visual and written frames, of the writer, and of the reader/viewer.

The text on page 118 elaborates on in-between themes and in-between languages that border on un-communicability, and the female narrator goes so close to the screen that she can no longer see the projected images. In both cases, one comes close to the medium at stake. In the first, the reader examines language in a new way, and in the second, the viewer becomes almost one with the screen. At the same time, this proximity with the medium also transports one outside of the representational frame, when one starts thinking beyond standard linguistic and filmic structures and thus achieves hybrid visions that can, at times, hinder understanding. In that case, an erotic movement in and out of the medium takes place. This in-between framing device appears physically in the text as well, when Cha uses language to describe a film sequence, and when she organizes her prose spatially, dissecting her text as one would cut a film to produce cross-cutting montage (see figure 17). Cha fragments her narrative so that we read alternating, detailed scenes on the struggles of a woman to express herself, a forced marriage, and the movements of a female character in a film. This technique derives from Sergei Eisenstein's film theory, in which he explains how the juxtaposition of two shots constructs meaning. In literature, the juxtaposed passages that do not follow a logical progression force us to make choices in how we read the section. We can either read every page according to the chronological page order, or temporarily exclude parts of the narrative, making a cut to follow the story line. This aesthetic device forces us to absorb language differently and to lose control over its progression because we unsettle the conventional ways of reading texts. Whether we decide to read it in the chronological page order or to skip sections, we make choices to access the best understanding of the text. Regardless of our choice, we either exclude parts of the narrative or disrupt the logic of the ordering of the text, even if only momentarily.

One can find similar experimental typographies in Sukenick's *Long Talking Bad Conditions Blues* and Federman's *Double or Nothing*. In Sukenick's work, typographical explorations are "generated by the activity of composition in an ongoing interchange between the mind and the page," so that his novels become open forms constantly improvised (*In Form* 8). Pages 26 through 41 in *Long Talking Bad Conditions Blues* look like Cha's work: large areas of white space alternate with text. Federman is another author who plays with the symmetry of pages, visual frames, and shapes of white spaces inside or along blocks of text. Federman's visual representation of the encasement of writing in boxed portions of texts expresses his

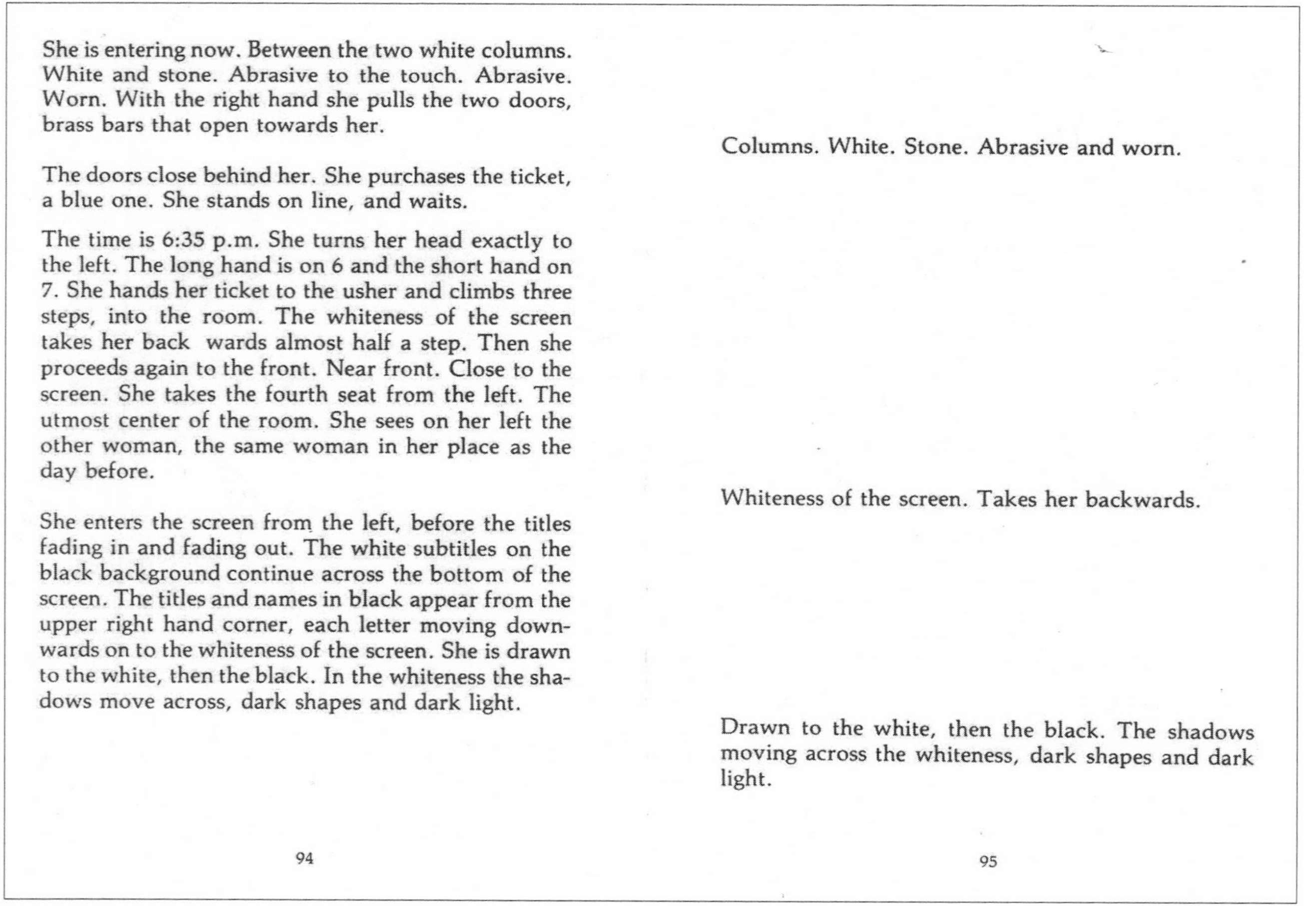

She is entering now. Between the two white columns. White and stone. Abrasive to the touch. Abrasive. Worn. With the right hand she pulls the two doors, brass bars that open towards her.

The doors close behind her. She purchases the ticket, a blue one. She stands on line, and waits.

The time is 6:35 p.m. She turns her head exactly to the left. The long hand is on 6 and the short hand on 7. She hands her ticket to the usher and climbs three steps, into the room. The whiteness of the screen takes her back wards almost half a step. Then she proceeds again to the front. Near front. Close to the screen. She takes the fourth seat from the left. The utmost center of the room. She sees on her left the other woman, the same woman in her place as the day before.

She enters the screen from the left, before the titles fading in and fading out. The white subtitles on the black background continue across the bottom of the screen. The titles and names in black appear from the upper right hand corner, each letter moving downwards on to the whiteness of the screen. She is drawn to the white, then the black. In the whiteness the sha-dows move across, dark shapes and dark light.

Columns. White. Stone. Abrasive and worn.

Whiteness of the screen. Takes her backwards.

Drawn to the white, then the black. The shadows moving across the whiteness, dark shapes and dark light.

FIGURE 17. Theresa Hak Kyung Cha. *DICTEE* pp. 94–95 (c) 2001 The Regents of the University of California. The University of California Press.

obsession with other modes of entrapment—closets, boxes, cubicles, and closed interior spaces. This visual and verbal exploration of confinement evokes Cha's own preoccupation with the physical, psychological, and linguistic oppressions that enclose women. Her approach differs from Federman's and Sukenick's in that her white gaps never fit the written blocks on her page. Thus, the reader cannot go from one narrative to the next as in Federman's and Sukenick's novels. The paginal experiments of *Long Talking Bad Conditions Blues* and *Double or Nothing* do not modify our reading technique as much as they interrupt it. Cha adds another layer of visual play as, in *DICTEE*, although the fragments of the text do not fit, their formal presentation does: each line on the facing pages is placed in the white space in-between the other two blocks of text. So while the reading process Cha sets up leads us to conclude that our relationship to language and narrative is unavoidably exclusive, her visual organization counterbalances this interpretation. In that sense, the interpretation of *DICTEE* itself remains "in-between" because Cha insists on keeping contradictory modes of writing. In exploring these various media and in mixing their conventions, Cha forces us to think about the rules of representation that distinguish each medium, but in linking them, she reveals that the best understanding of her text literally takes place "in-between." This is why Cha insists that boundaries are "*Un imaginable*" (87). Cha plays with the French word "un," the masculine pronoun meaning "one" and "a" so that, in cutting the word "unimaginable," the phrase "un imaginable" could mean, in a bilingual mode, "one imaginable" boundary. At the same time, "unimaginable" is also present in this bilingual phrase so that the boundaries are both imaginable and unimaginable.

This in-between mode results from Cha's conception of language's bodily origin. As Karmen MacKendrick reminds us, language and the body engage an "odd doubleness": "Both are in some sense *me*—my material self, my descriptions, my voice—and yet both are precisely what link me—more, what make me a conduit—to the outside" (109). As a matter of fact, language is articulated through the mouth, a gateway between the inside and outside of the body, which leads Cha to eroticize language as an in-between material. To that end, *DICTEE* builds recurring images of bodily fluids and orifices. In her examination of images of penetrations and punctures, birthing, and speech processes, and the recurrence of the mouth, vaginal canals, and skin as loci of absorption and permeability, Juliana Chang notes that the "liquid tongue saliva [is a] site of dissolution, disintegration. making [*sic*] fluid so as to flow into absorption, incorporation" (Chang "Transform" 78). The images of "dissolution," "disintegration," "absorption," and "incorporation" repeat in the text, which leads Chang to assert that *DICTEE* is a metaphor of a body. The image of blood, for example, recurs, as Cha makes a parallel between blood and ink: "the image of blood, punctured from the skin, flowing and gushing from the veins, splattered on paper, becoming stain, like writing, or rather, becoming writing itself" (Shih 153). In a scene in which the narrator donates blood, the narration focuses on the in-between-ness of the cotton. The cotton becomes a contact zone (see figure 18):

> She takes my left arm, tells me to make a fist, then open. Make a fist then open again, make the vein appear through the skin blue-green-purple tint to the translucent surface. Pump them open and close. She takes the elastic band and ties it tightly around the left arm. She taps on the flesh presses against it her thumb. She removes the elastic to the right arm. Open and close the right hand, fist and palm. She takes the cotton and rubs alcohol lengthwise on the arm several times. The coolness disappears as the liquid begins to evaporate. She takes the needle with its empty body to the skin.

FIGURE 18. Theresa Hak Kyung Cha. *DICTEE* p. 64 (c) 2001 The Regents of the University of California. The University of California Press.

Note Cha's choice of words, emphasizing the in-between-ness of the body: "open," "surface," "pump," "open and close." The boundaries between interior and exterior realms become progressively blurred. In fact, as Benthien notes, our conception of skin is dual: it is "either a closed, protective layer or a permeable, transparent membrane" (143). Cha explores both aspects of skin in the above passage: the nurse tells the narrator to make a fist and open. This activity then transfers to the inside of the left arm, as the pumping action is attributed to the vein and the fist. Eventually, in referring to the "empty body" of the needle, Cha blurs even more the distinction between the inside and outside of the body (see figure 19).

Cha reverses the standard role we give to materials: we usually conceive of materials as something that absorbs a stain. Here, the stain absorbs the cotton square. In changing the customary action of absorption, Cha reveals the limits of our habitual understandings. Her challenge of these usual conceptions includes our comprehension of the boundary between the body and language, as Cha switches from "sang" (blood) to "encre" (ink), allowing

Stain begins to absorb the material spilled on.

She pushes hard the cotton square against the mark.

Stain begins to absorb the material spilled on.

Something of the ink that resembles the stain from the interior emptied onto emptied into emptied upon this boundary this surface. More. Others. When possible ever possible to puncture to scratch to imprint. Expel. Ne te cache pas. Révèle toi. Sang. Encre. Of its body's extention of its containment.

FIGURE 19. Theresa Hak Kyung Cha. *DICTEE* p. 65 (c) 2001 The Regents of the University of California. The University of California Press.

leakage between the written and the bodily. In English, "sang" is associated with the singing act, which highlights the expressiveness of the body since blood and singing are joined. In addition, as Carol Moe points out, "with the misspelling of extension, Cha plays on the word 'extent.' She refers to what is within the extent of the body and to what extends beyond the body" (66). In blurring the boundaries between the cotton and the stain and ink and blood, Cha shows that "neither language nor the body turns out to be containers or able to contain" (Moe 65). This allows the creation of a new body, "Immaterial [. . .] and formless, having surrendered to dissolution limb by limb, all parts that compose a body," which illustrates the in-between-ness of the Third Body (161). Through a re-conceptualization of the roles and representations of the body within patriarchal and national frameworks, Cha calls for new reading modes, an aspect of *écriture féminine* that is lacking in Cixous's work. In *DICTEE,* the fluid female identity, combined with the polysemy of Cha's words, images, and the reflections on the materials used to document women's lives, "opens" Cha's work: there is no abstracting distance between the reader and the text. In other words, we cannot always presume to know what the words and images refer to, and thus we cannot master the meaning of the text, which settles the erotic mode of reading *DICTEE* calls for.

This erotic mode is rooted in geographical movements, gender delimitations, and political boundaries: blood, saliva, and body orifices are loci of penetrations, exchanges, and changes.[15] Spahr shows that "the blood

15. For more detailed readings of the blood scene in relation to nationality and race, see Berila's *The Art of Change: Experimental Writing, Cultural Activism, and Feminist Social Transformation.*

with its metaphoric relation to wholes of nationality, race, and gender becomes instead a 'hole' that assimilates the boundaries" (Spahr *Connective 5*). Hence, "*DICTEE* [is] a text of immigration, as a work that absorbs and takes on other places as its own" (Spahr *Connective 5*). Cha's erotic approach to absorption and boundaries reveals that issues of exile, immigration, race, and power are deeply engaged in matters of sexual identity, gender, and erotics. Such erotic expressions are not distinct from *DICTEE's* geopolitical matters because "racialization, sexualization, and genderization of female corporeality" "become crucial sites of exploration" of "notions such as country, homeland, region, locality, and ethnicity" (Kaplan, Alarcón, and Moallem 14). As Amal Amireh and Lisa Suhair Majaj remind us, "Many feminists have argued that nationalist ideology is inherently masculinist, imposing a burden of cultural transmission and the role of national signifier upon women while reinforcing 'a definable [generally oppressive] gender regime' (Kandiyoti 376, 378)" (89). The erotic openness of Cha's work allows readers to realize, through their reading activity, that

> geographies of belonging and displacement need not be positioned as narrowly nationalist or bounded; rather, they can be mobilized within local spaces that attend to the racism and orientalism of (sexual) consumption by engaging practices that are analytic, political, and cultural, that are at once relational, synergistic and generous. (Alexander 88)

In *DICTEE,* the eroticization of the dissolution of the Korean nation and of female identities reveals the interconnectedness and interdependence of geographic and political conflicts and of the erotic practices that puncture bodies and nations. Such interconnectedness and interdependence are (re)negotiated through erotic/linguistic loci of exchanges that, like the Third Body, are in-between sites of struggle. Cha also "creates and celebrates a kind of third space, an exile space that becomes a source of individual vision and power. Indeed, far from dropping a specific identity in favor of endless difference, she predicts the breakdown of binaries that are part of the logic of domination" (Kim 8). As other critics have revealed, this political third space is a place of conflict on a postcolonial level, as it allows a critique of the West's domination, but as I have shown, it is also a feminist locus of positive creation—the "*Pleasure in the image pleasure in the copy pleasure in the projection of likeness pleasure in the repetition*" (17). Consequently, the postcolonial resistance highlighted in many critiques of *DICTEE* is not distinct from the linguistic rhythms and the textual materials that express the pulses and bodily actions of the Third Body.

Cha's exploration of the Third Body proposes a new knowledge of corporeality that unsettles the rules and values nation-states rely on, while generating an alternative sensual and transnational mode of knowing through our engagement with the medium of the text. In breaking down the binary opposition between body and language, Cha invites her readers to relate sensually to her verbalized thoughts. Through our participation in her text, the distinction between subject and object becomes blurred in an erotic embrace. Cha insists on the porous boundaries of reading and writing through her phrasing of "the interior emptied onto emptied into emptied upon this boundary this surface." This in-between relation is not simple, however, as "the blood is not merely drawn into the needle but the 'interior' is 'emptied onto' (a spilling out towards the boundary/surface), 'emptied into' (becoming a part of and mixing with the boundary/surface), and 'emptied upon' (a placing on top of and a closeness to the boundary/surface)" (Spahr "Postmodernism"). Therefore, Cha's theory of reading blurs the boundaries between the reader and the text and invites multiple interactions with the text (onto, into, upon), allowing linguistic foreplay.

This reading is pleasurable because, as Barthes explains, "My pleasure can very well take the form of a drift. *Drifting* occurs whenever *I do not respect the whole*" (*Pleasure* 18). The unfinished quality of the text allows readers to attend to its abrasions and ruptures (Ott "(Re)locating" 204). During such interactions with the material of language the reader comes to experience a non-*thetic* moment when his or her ego and the book become one. Consequently, our deciphering of *DICTEE* relies not only on our intellect but also on our bodily relationship with the material of the text. Words and images thus become erotic *materials*. Cha, in calling attention to such materials, demands that we examine their roles and effects on literary interpretation. Tomasula makes this a central matter in *VAS*. In the next chapter, I will turn to his invitation to physically engage the reader with textual and visual media, and I will elaborate on the pleasurable politics that derive from this invitation.

FIGURE 20. Steve Tomasula. *VAS: An Opera in Flatland* Cover (c) 2004 Steve Tomasula. The University of Chicago Press.

chapter five

Bodily and Literary Modifications in Steve Tomasula's *VAS: An Opera in Flatland*

The cover of *VAS: An Opera in Flatland* posits Tomasula's interest in the materiality of literature: the novel looks like a punctured and tattooed body cradled in the reader's hand. The chromosome code that interrupts the title is pressed into the skin of the book, its color in contrast with the red letters of the title and of the author's and designer's names. These letters are composed of round drops that resemble blood; they could also be the letters of a fresh tattoo that, in irritating the skin, has left a blushed shade surrounding the letters, like the reflections of a small neon sign that draws attention to its presence. As we open the book, a page colored with a dark red similar to the letters on the cover allows us to "'peel back the skin to the blood' underneath," so that, "vas," which is Latin for "vessel," specifically one for transmitting fluids, literally transports blood. (Farrell qdt. in Vanderborg 11). This prepares the reader for the exploration of bodily matters that follows—documents about eugenics, tables of comparisons of cranial measurements and Miss America measurements since 1921, medical imaging, egg and sperm commercialization websites, IQ tests, biology patents, excerpts from anatomy, history, and natural history books, aesthetic surgery advertisements, newspaper articles, and a 25-page reproduction of chromosome 12 code.

These documents interrelate with the life of Square, a writer whose wife suggests that he have a vasectomy after she has a miscarriage and an abortion. During his discussion with his wife, Circle, his mother-in-law, and his daughter, Oval, and while he is thinking about the "procedure," Square evokes the problems linked to body changes and rewritings, and asks questions about the ethics of vasectomy, eugenics, forced sterilizations, and body modifications. The narration and the collage of documents are aligned with a single margin-line that separates the main text from the occasional marginal comments. At times, margin-lines and typefaces are multiplied, so that our interpretation of the novel relies on its presentation as much as its content. This research in textual and visual materiality interrogates the technology that produces it and "mobilizes reflexive loops between [the novel's] imaginative world and the material apparatus embodying that creation as a physical presence" (Hayles *Writing Machine* 25). These kinds of reflections imply a correlation between the material body and the text.

The insertion of the body in the book comes from Tomasula's wish to use "the space of the page as part of the novel: in this case, the physical body of the book (body text) is used as a metaphor for the human body, just as human bodies, which can be written, coded, rearranged (a more literal kind of body text), can be seen as a metaphor for the book" ("Multimedia Writing"). This is particularly clear at the end of the opera section, which appears at the end of the book as a cartoon about the evolution of humankind. Page 359 depicts an ape whose arteries are sutured. The ape's transplant mirrors the transplant of the cartoon onto the novel. The appearance of the book is close to that of skin: the red page compares to bloody skin on which an operation is performed. Consequently, while this skin is modified through an operation, the book itself changes during this cartoon section: it is a separate part that does not follow the usual design of the novel (with the vertical margin-lines, the narrative, the quotes, and images). We go back to the regular format of the novel on page 365, when the book returns to Square's operation. Such treatment of congruent modifications of body and text calls for our interaction with the medium of the novel, which forces us to consider reading as a physical activity. Here, Tomasula's insistence on the physicality of reading has affinities with McElroy's, Maso's, and Cha's projects, as he also points to the verbal and/or visual materials of fiction. In *VAS*, the exploration of textual materiality is more pragmatic, however, since the book appears quite literally as a body.

Tomasula's other works also explore body art, new reproduction technologies, and body modifications. He has produced critical essays on genetic art and on the relationship between image and text in contemporary literature.[1] This dual interest has led him to write *In&Oz* (2003), "a novel of Art, Love, Auto Mechanics" that elaborates on the connections between mechanical repairs and human lives. The multimedia novel *TOC* (2009) explores time—the invention of the second, the beating of a heart, humans' spiritual and everyday use of time, and the history of humans' past and future—in text, film, music, photography, speech, animation, and painting ("Steve Tomasula"). *The Book of Portraiture* (2006) is "a postmodern epic in writing and images" about how we represent ourselves, thereby shaping the definitions of humanity ("Steve Tomasula"). While *The Book of Portraiture* focuses on modes of portraiture, *VAS* explores the modes of modification humans have used to transform their bodies. In *VAS,* Tomasula collaborates with Stephen Farrell, a graphic artist, designer, and typographer who has produced imagetext collaborations and multimedia exhibits. They use historical representations of the body to reflect on how texts and human bodies have been represented and rearranged throughout time.

Because of the novel's involvement in the technological aspects of prints and body modifications, critics often interpret *VAS* as a book that comments on the impact of technology on our lives. Anna Everett and John T. Caldwell claim that *VAS*'s exploration of the "conjunctions of (fictional and nonfictional) narrative and image [. . .] amounts to a collision between scientific discourse and fictive meditation " (260). Thus, "Jay David Bolter and Richard Grusin's recent work on remediation is apt to provide a more bracing account of Tomasula's achievement than might be had using current literary-theoretical models" (260). Remediation is the use of a medium within another medium. In *VAS,* the representation of web pages in the fiction is an example of remediation. Everett and Caldwell imply that the mix of fictional and factual media results in a transformation of the fictional mode that pushes the boundaries of traditional literary criticism. Within this framework, they add, "Whether in fact the primary aim of (Tomasula's) hypermediacy is to effect immediacy will perhaps be the occasion for future disquisition" (260). Answering their call, I wish to draw from remediation

1. See "Gene(sis)" in *Data Made Flesh: Embodying Information,* eds. Robert Mitchell and Phillip Thurtle (New York: Routledge, 2003); "Genetic Art and the Aesthetics of Biology" in *Leonardo* (MIT Press) 35, No. 2 (2002); and "Art in the Age of the Individual's Mechanical Reproduction" in *The New Art Examiner* 25, No. 7 (April 1998). For information on word and image creations, refer to "Ways of Seeing / Ways of Being" in the *Electronic Book Review,* No. 7 (Winter 1997–98) and "Multimedia Writing."

theory to study *VAS* in order to discover the consequences of Tomasula's use of various media on our reading experience.

David Bolter and Richard Grusin's remediation theory postulates that, in absorbing other media, remediation strives for immediacy, or that which allows the medium to disappear, immersing the viewer in a visual world that is as close as possible to daily visual experiences. The logic of immediacy "dictates that the medium itself should disappear and leave us in the presence of the thing represented" (6). For example, a video embedded in a website relies on immediacy, as it gives access to live recording. But in order to achieve this effect of immediacy, the webcam footage has to be framed and presented, so that it is only a window in a website that combines various media (print, film, photographs). In presenting the webcam, the website relies on hypermediacy, or that which emphasizes the process of performance and construction of the media, making "us aware of the medium or media and (in sometimes subtle and sometimes obvious ways) reminding us of our desire for immediacy" (34). The various windows that construct the website strive to reach a real experience, but they all depend on each other because they "define themselves by the standards of the media they are trying to erase" (54). The interdependence of the two logics relies on the fact that "Although each medium promises to reform its predecessors by offering a more immediate or authentic experience, the promise of reform inevitably leads us to become aware of the new medium as a medium" (19). Consequently, viewers always fluctuate between a sense of loss of awareness of the construction of the medium and an awareness of its artificiality in visual texts, specifically, film, web media, and video games, where immediacy and hypermediacy play important roles.

Artists play with our desire for immediacy when they refuse to present the mediation transparently. In hypermediacy, artists emphasize the process and constructed-ness of the medium they are using, thus critiquing and refashioning it. In the later part of *VAS* (237 forward), we encounter examples of remediation through the reproduction of the web medium into the textual medium. One can find similar uses of shots of computer screens in Lee Seigel's *Love in a Dead Country,* where they interrelate with the Kama Sutra narrative (156–64). Much like in Seigel's novel, *VAS* includes images of Netscape® windows and ad boxes, including actual companies' advertisements: My Twinn® creates a twin doll of the customer's child; Stratagene® is a biological research company "developing innovative products and technologies for life science research"; Beckman Coulter specializes in biomedical research and clinical diagnosis; New England Biolabs "offers the largest selection of recombinant and native enzymes for genomic research"; Operon is "the global market leader in high volume synthesis and provider of quality DNA oligonucleotides and array-ready oligo sets or AROS"; and so forth ("Stratagene"; "New England Biolabs"; "Operon"). These websites are used as collage material, mixed with previous visual patterns from earlier stages of the novel, such as the musical clef (255, the repetition of the scar on page 263 echoing page [158], and the appearance of the typeface used to write chromosome 12 code ([201–26]). Here, remediation occurs, as a new medium is created through the combination of the web media and of the textual references throughout the book (265).

This remediation involves immediacy and hypermediacy since there is a constant coming and going between the immersion of the reader in Square's story and the realization—a moment of hypermediacy—of the construction of the information presented to him or her. This often occurs when Square is relating an incident and technical data interrupts the narrative about his life. For example, while Square is at the Fourth of July parade with Oval and Circle, he watches an anti-abortion float on which "A man dressed like the Grim / Reaper pantomimed hacking through its umbilical / cord with a scythe" (117). After someone throws a water balloon at the Grim Reaper, he rushes toward Circle, "pointing his scythe directly at the balloon in / her hand" ([118]). Circle asks Square to do something, and after he reacts with a "Huh?" and Oval throws candies at the Grim Reaper, the narration ends on these words: "The dog launched / itself into the Grim Reaper's black robes. Snarling, / it shook him violently" (119). The text then shifts to "regarding mollusks, there are over 100,000 varieties," and the story resumes on the next page ("'well what did you want me to do?' Square / protested on the way home."), after a quote by Herman Muller and J. B. S. Haldane ([120]):

Regarding people, as Hermann Muller,
geneticist and 1962 Nobel Laureate put it:
Probably close to 20 percent of the population . . . have inherited a genetic
defect. . . . To avoid genetic degeneration, then, that 20 percent should not
be allowed to reach sexual maturity.
     The difference being that differences in mollusks were
seen as variation not deformity and classifying them—
     As J. B. S. Haldane said of eliminating human variation,
Once you deem it desirable to begin, it is a little difficult to know where
you are to stop. (119)

While the quotes and the plot are loosely connectable—they both deal with the control of human sexuality and the issues that the control of reproduction entails—they are not explicitly related, and more importantly, the factual information of the quotes interrupts Square's story. The pause in the narrative allows us to feel inside and then outside of the fiction, as we shift from a fictional to a factual framework when going from the narrative to quotes or charts. This play on immediacy and hypermediacy reveals that, as Everett and Caldwell suggest, "the primary aim of (Tomasula's) hypermediacy is to effect immediacy" (260).

Indeed, *VAS* transgresses the rhetoric of remediation, which relies on the assumption that new media reform previous (and weaker) ones. Bolter and Grusin note that "the word remediation is used by educators as a euphemism for the task of bringing lagging students up to an expected level of performance and by environmental engineers for 'restoring' a damaged ecosystem. The word derives ultimately from the Latin remederi—to 'heal, to restore health'" (59). Thus, Bolter and Grusin have adopted the word remediation "to express the way in which one medium is seen by our culture as reforming or improving upon another" (59). Because the development of new media is assumed to bring us closer to the experience of reality, "the rhetoric of remediation favors immediacy and transparency, even though as the medium matures it offers new opportunities for hypermediacy" (60). *VAS* resists this rhetoric, as it "rejects the traditional notion of typography as a transparent medium for the writer's thoughts" (Poynor). As Rick Poynor adds, "the effect of reading such a book is to be constantly reminded, with every page turn, that this is what [we are] doing." This self-awareness allows the reader to rethink the vehicles of different discourses. Because the novel also deals with various modes of remediation thematically—medical remedies, social reforms, media evolution, and bodily repairs—Tomasula questions remediation as reform both in his treatment of textual media and in his political questions about the ethics of genetics, sterilization, and body modifications. As we shall see, this double focus prevents the reader from separating erotic configurations of media and the political rethinking that they trigger.

Such rethinking occurs when, for example, Tomasula reproduces an information card of a painting by Charles Willson Peale from the Pennsylvania Academy of the Fine Arts. The card appears on a black background that resembles the glass of a copy machine. On the card, under the painting's information, we read, "MAY NOT BE REPRODUCED WITHOUT PERMISSION" (327). Davis Schneiderman comments on this humorous moment:

[T]he placard that presumably describes the painting, clearly emblazoned with the words "MAY NOT BE REPRODUCED WITHOUT PERMISSION" (327) becomes a part of the new text—in fact meeting the citation requirement while simultaneously de-realizing the warning of the card, which, with its injunction against reproduction, obviously refers to the reproduction of the painting, and not the reference card. ("Notes")

As Schneiderman points out, the card becomes part of a new medium, *VAS,* and Tomasula's playful observation on reproduction regulations triggers reflection about which materials are reproducible and what immediacy attempts to hide. This disruption of immediacy always reminds us of our reading activity and of the ways in which we adapt to the shift of the frameworks and metafictional devices in the novel.

While Tomasula disturbs the immediacy effect, he also uses remediation to compose a novel where the narrative, quotes, and data oddly build on one another. Indeed, the interrupting data often offer a way back into the fiction, or new outlooks on it. On the other hand, the fictional events also provide a different perspective on the scientific and technical information. In the first sentence of the narrative, we read, "Then knowledge: a paper cut," which relates to Square's writing activity and his thoughts on knowledge in relation to writing ([10]). The material characteristics of print documents are emphasized since the next paragraph begins with "on the page on his lap," and the next page shows the print of a patient's form with Square's first name handwritten in the designated boxes. Tomasula's insertion of administrative forms in Square's story evokes the metafictional games of novels such as Federman's *Take It or Leave It,* which includes a questionnaire. Halfway through Federman's novel, the narrative pauses to survey the reader's opinion on the novel: "1. Up to here have you liked the recitation? YES [ ] No [ ]." The mode of writing and presentation of the questionnaire draws attention to what we take for granted in the fictional form, style, and typography. The content of the twelve questions also sheds light on the constructedness of the book. Tomasula shares Federman's metafictional strategies: his remediation of other media in the realm of writing takes Federman's stylistic and print experimentations to another level of awareness of the contrivances of fiction-writing.

In Tomasula's work, this awareness is presented in the context of the work of Edwin A. Abbott, whose words appear on the page facing Square's form: "Imagine a vast sheet of paper on which straight Lines, Triangles, / Squares, Pentagons, Hexagons, and other figures move freely about" ([12]). The quote allows the reader to make a direct connection between the material qualities of *VAS* and *Flatland*. Abbott's 1884 science fiction novella *Flatland: A Romance of Many Dimensions* offers satirical observations on social hierarchy. In the novella, Square lives in a two-dimensional world and regards two-dimensional structures as the *only* societal structure. When Square discovers the existence of a third dimension, he becomes aware of the social contradictions of his world, and reflects on institutionally organized structures, dimensions, and hierarchies.

On page [12] of *VAS*, while Abbott's words interrupt Square's story, they also enrich it because they allow intertextual connections between Abbott's and Tomasula's works. As I will argue in this chapter, this quote sets up Tomasula's play with the idea of *VAS* itself as being a "vast sheet of paper on which straight lines, Triangles, / Squares, Pentagons, Hexagons, and other figures move freely about." This idea allows him to engage the reader in an interaction with the visual organization of information, allocating him or her a performative position of a political activity through a palpable reading. To substantiate this position, first the relationship between *VAS* and *Flatland* must be clarified.

There are obvious similarities between the world of *VAS* and *Flatland*. Indeed, numerous reviewers have noted that *VAS*'s characters, much like *Flatland*'s, "are, quite literally, flat," and Tomasula himself stresses Flatlanders' "depressingly / narrow semiotics of product" (Poynor; *VAS* 31).[2] Such flatness relies on the two-dimensional principal of Flatland:

> *Imagine a penny on a table*, Square remembered thinking
> the first time he set eyes on Flatland.
> [. . .]
> *But if you gradually bring your eye down to the level of the table top,*
> *it becomes a line and this is how I and the other inhabitants of Flatland*
> *appear to each other.* ([34]–35)

In *Flatland*, Square guides the reader through the implications of two-dimensional life. In using Abbott's concept, Tomasula emphasizes the inability of any society to conceive of the unnaturalness of their social paradigms because they take them for granted. In *VAS*, Circle has "a / heritage of genes giving her face and body proportions that happened to be in vogue / at their moment in history"; the measurements of the beauty pageants have evolved following what was "in vogue" throughout history, and so forth (17, 238). In reminding us of what is "in vogue" and in

---

2. See reviews by Emily Pérez, Kass Fleisher, Eugene Thacker, and Poynor.

using hypermediacy, Tomasula shows the constructed-ness of any social discourse, including literature. For example, a target appears in the middle of black dots, reminding us of the dots on page [187], themselves repeating page [151]. They also echo the form to fill out on page [38]. This target reappears on page 232 without the dots and with the inscription "No Exit" in the middle of it. The variation on visual themes forces us not only to connect the various parts of the book in a moment of hypermediacy but also to explore the visual media and the connotations of each variation. The appearance of the text itself shows that "The word is made flesh not as a voice, not as a score, an image, an icon, or an event but as a text whose visual properties and idiosyncrasies enact themselves for the eye, upon the page" (Drucker *Figuring* 109). This word "made flesh" makes us self-aware of our reading experience, while pointing out the ways in which values and rules are socially constructed: "No Exit" confirms that there is no way out of Flatland. Consequently, an escape from Flatland as pictured in Abbott's novel does not occur.

More specifically, Circle does not have the power to deracinate Square from his Flatland, as "*VAS* playfully makes its own Circle a woman and a powerful lawyer. But this ostensibly feminist strategy raises the memory of older essentializing stereotypes of curvy, cycle-driven females, and *VAS*'s Circle is continually fending off criticism of her reproductive decisions from a mother who urges her to fulfill herself by bearing a new baby" (Vanderborg 6). As Susan Vanderborg indicates, the conflict between Circle's "emancipation" and the inescapability from the stereotypes of her society reveals that escaping the logic of one's Flatland may not be as practical as Abbott implies. Vanderborg also suggests that "the queries and smudges may not quite release us from Flatland, but they offer a more honest survey of our struggles to record and generate new evolutionary texts, that 'species of free verse Darwin / had helped midwife, so long ago' (179)" (10). In that sense, the characters inhabiting *VAS*'s Flatland are more cynical about the possibility for transcendence than are Abbott's Flatlanders. Indeed, up until the end of the novel, we do not find a resolution to the questions *VAS* asks. Square ends up on the operating table, waiting for the vasectomy to be performed, but Tomasula does not relate the operation. We decide, in the end, whether Square's DNA will be added to future generations' or whether he will get a vasectomy. What is ironic is that, in both cases, he will take part in the development of humanity: in the first case, he will contribute to DNA evolution, and in the second, he will follow the new trend to control fertility. In both situations, he will still be part of his Flatland, "the Land of the 1001 Salad Dressings" ([120]).

The casualness of the last scene emphasizes the inescapability from Flatland, since the surgeon, while preparing his scalpels, complains about the choice of music in the office. Ironically, the music associated with procreation is the vasectomy surgeon's favorite: the doctor shares Circle's mother's taste in opera, and he would rather perform vasectomies listening to Wagner (Vanderborg 9). This humorous final scene, which is supposed to be the climax of Square's story, only reminds us that we are reading "a common story / [. . .] So common that many people / wouldn't even consider it a story. / [. . .] So common that its commonness was the story" ([18]–19). The narrative, which at first seemed to be a compensation for the cut Square was expecting, ends up compensating for an operation that does not actually happen in the novel. At that point, however, we have long realized that what matters most is not Square's decision, which remains trapped in the modes of thinking of his society, but rather the problems his investigation reveals. This implies that any society, including the reader's, will remain blind to its societal biases and considers them natural rules when they are in fact social agreements. The realization that there is no way out of these social agreements leads the reader to understand the constructed-ness of any information.

Yet, as David Banash points out, "There is no narrative explanation of how we should read these different statements [the quotes in the novel]. They are presented simply as fragments which have a complex relationship to one another, as well as to the narrative as a whole" (22). Because VAS does not voice a moral concern when presenting disturbing information in its collage of quotes, it does not seem to denounce or resist any particular discourse, like formally innovative texts have often been thought to do. For Tomasula, merely opposing ideologies is not sufficient:

> I'm just trying to step back and take the big view and ask how has an attitude that sees the body as something that can be manipulated and collaged and rearranged, and have artificial parts put in, pacemakers and all this—how has this attitude developed, and what does it mean? (Tomasula, personal interview)

In asking such questions through competing viewpoints and plagiarized visual and written texts, Tomasula invites us to become more skeptical of any discourse's claim of authenticity, including his own. For instance, in his collage of websites specializing in new reproduction technologies, genetics, and biology research, he discloses that these companies omit ethical debates about the technologies they promote.

Such disclosure occurs, for instance, when we reach the photo of hair selection after reading about the technical aspects of body modifications, including forced sterilization (53–[54]), abortion (197), and radiation experiments ([252]):

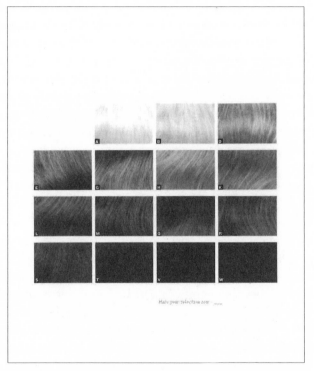

FIGURE 21. Steve Tomasula. *VAS: An Opera in Flatland* p. 236 (c) 2004 Steve Tomasula. The University of Chicago Press.

As opposed to the cartoon-like representations of the body that appear in earlier parts of the narrative ([22–23], 70, 161), the texture of the hair feels sensual, allowing us to experience the fascination of the person who would choose from these samples (see figure 21). Nevertheless, this fascination enables the reader to account for the manipulation of such devices. The sentence "Make your selection now: _ _ _" under the images of hair adds a technical and cold quality to the sensual image. The opposition between the attractive picture of beautiful hair and the sentence underneath it, as well as the letters referring to each hair section, renders the selection of hair less glamorous. As Vanderborg insightfully writes, such "montages that make us rethink our own acceptance of packaged images designed to deflect close scrutiny of how their forms or sales pitches were developed" (7). Hence, we are forced to think about what this selection implies; we have to rethink the illusion of empowerment these advertisements promote through their "hassle-free," shopper-oriented ordering procedures. More specifically, in the context of *VAS*'s genealogy of eugenics, "selection" evokes the German word "selektion," which refers to the process of selecting prisoners to be murdered in extermination camps. Here, the photos representing stocks of hair evoke the piles of human hair found in Nazi camps. Therefore, the images of glossy hair that are seemingly more reminiscent of boxes of hair-coloring products lining store shelves invite us to ponder the relationship between the horrors of Nazism and the capitalistic rationale of commodification prevailing in our contemporary societies.

While *VAS* fosters a rethinking of the implications of such rationales, it does so in a playful manner, so that textual pleasure takes part in our social examinations. For example, the playful use of tabs on the right-hand side of most pages of the book implies that the novel can be used as a dictionary or an encyclopedia, and that it can be read nonlinearly: instead of following the narrative thread about Square, one may follow the alphabetic listing of quotes. This nonlinear reading method is in line with other manipulations of reading methodologies. Siegel's *Love in a Dead Language,* for instance, includes upside-down pages, so the book must be rotated in the reading process. In such books we can approach a topic from different angles, and the nonlinear structure allows the mingling of various viewpoints. In *VAS,* on page 81, the tab suddenly appears at the center of the book (on the left-hand side), disrupting the usual organization of the book and making the tab useless. This forces us to extend our evaluation of the vehicles and structuring of information. Here, by surprising us, Tomasula calls our attention to the construction of the book and to any text using the tab device, reminding us that they are simply organizational tools that we have agreed on and accepted.

This leads us to further explore the connections between Tomasula's and Abbott's Flatlands: in crafting a visual book whose material challenges the linear qualities of writing, Tomasula ironically offers another kind of response to Abbott. While he refutes Abbott's idea that it is possible to transcend the narrowness of Flatland, the author produces a novel that breaks away from novel-writing conventions, redirecting our attention to the arrangement of the book's materials. We may not generally consider the material of novels to be as important as the message they carry, but *VAS* insists that we reconsider the ways in which we interact with a text's materiality. The importance of the materiality of the book is obvious when an image of *VAS*'s page (with its typical vertical lines) becomes inserted into the actual page of the book, as if the data usually inscribed in the page have taken over the control of information, inscribing Square's thoughts within their medical wanderings (273) (see figure 22). This change invites us to consider more closely the layout of the book: it allows us to play with modes of representation. In challenging us with an unusual presentation of information and in forcing us to take part in a playful engagement with the text that resists hierarchy, Tomasula "teach[es] people how to read, [not just] novels, but read the world" (Tomasula, personal interview). Responses to *VAS* have revealed that such reading lessons rely on a disturbance of traditional reading methods. Reviewers feel that "26 pages of gene sequencing [. . .] comes off merely as intellectually lazy," or "truly unreadable," and that, in the novel, "it may have been comforting to some readers to have a few moments of absolute stability" (Flake; *Literary Saloon;* Pérez). Others are "intrigued by Tomasula's work, simply because it asks the reader how to read" (Thacker 166). Such reactions about what constitutes a "readable" book reflect the concerns of *VAS* itself, which is to always question its status. What frustrates or satisfies readers is that our reading process relies not only on the deciphering of a message but also on an immersion in the material of the text. Indeed, the tabs hint at the possibility of reading the book in various ways, or even of skipping parts of the book, such as the two pages of footnotes, pages [90] through 91.

Tomasula's humorous use of footnotes pays homage to novels, such as Vladimir Nabokov's *Pale Fire,* that insert footnotes to unsettle narrative techniques: the notes wittingly tug at the main "plot" and ridicule their very existence. In *VAS,* footnotes 14 through 16 on page 90 are footnotes to footnotes that mock notes' claim to authority. Yet, the accumulation of notes does not just undermine the "main" narrative of the novel; it also overwhelms the reader with sources of information, much as in Mark Danielewski's *House of Leaves,* which, in combining a mass of information and lengthy notes, immerses the reader in a claustrophobic realm that mirrors the confusing world of the characters. Like Tomasula's novel, *The House of Leaves* underlines the contrivances of its narrative through a presentation of competing sources, typefaces, and narrative devices. While Danielewski's novel focuses on such contrivances to write a satire of academic criticism, *VAS* does so to show the ways in which texts, like bodies, are written and modified in accord with social trends and evolutions. Thus, *VAS* invites readers to adapt to the "swamp" of information on bodily matters, while at the same time reflecting on the limitations of the organization of the very book they are reading (Tomasula, personal interview).

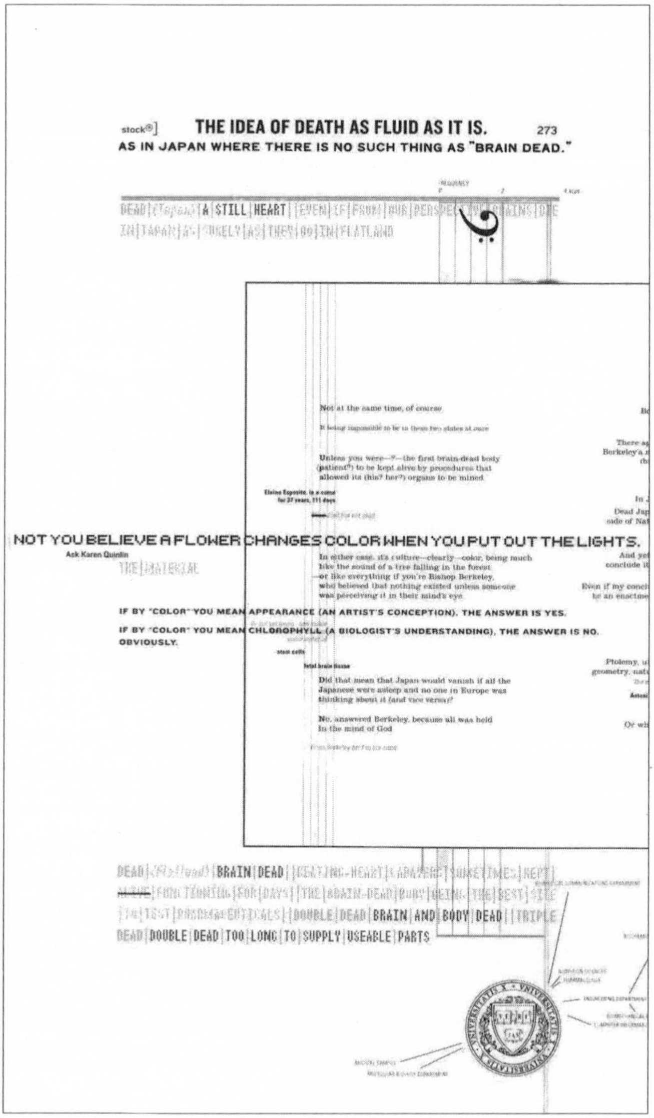

FIGURE 22. Steve Tomasula. *VAS: An Opera in Flatland* p. 273 (c) 2004 Steve Tomasula. The University of Chicago Press.

This interest in the book as a material object invites us to ponder how visual and social constructions frame and define a medium and its evolution. Indeed, Tomasula "want[s] the text itself to be seen as a material object," so that when reading *VAS*, we are constantly reminded that we hold a book in our hands (personal interview). We read, for example, "Body text once had body? [. . .] Couldn't it again?" This question is inserted within an illumination, reminding us of the visual changes in writing: the aestheticization of writing once accepted as a norm has now disappeared (see figure 23).

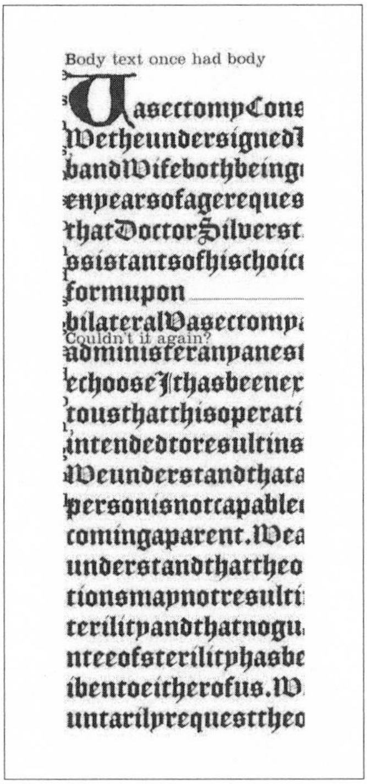

FIGURE 23. Steve Tomasula. *VAS: An Opera in Flatland* p. 51 (c) 2004 Steve Tomasula. The University of Chicago Press.

The complex patterns and designs of illuminations once expressed visually the theme and mood of the text, while also embracing the artistic codes of the text's time and culture. Now that illuminations are no longer used, printing procedures and circulation processes have standardized the arrangement of words on a page. Tomasula's reinsertion of illuminations in contemporary typography evokes the opening of William Gass's *Willie Masters' Lonesome Wife*, where a naked woman holds a wooden piece shaped as an "s," the first letter of the text. As H. L. Hix notes, Gass disrupts the tradition of illuminated manuscripts that used angels or virgins in their handwritten drawings (65). Instead, Gass provides a picture of his protagonist, Babs, bending toward the letter, as if ready to eat it. The suggestive pause foreshadows the sexual and humoristic tone of the book, while setting up the metaphor of writing and reading as intercourse. Tomasula does not recall the use of illumination to establish a pornographic narrative, but like Gass, he asks his reader to think about why the arrangement of print has become unimportant in fiction writing.

What we have excluded from our reading may in fact disclose the most valuable tools of acquiring knowledge. As we read *VAS*, our interaction with textual materiality is as important as our interpretation of its data. Thus, the novel leads us to reconsider what dominant reading techniques have excluded from reading practices as much as it leads us to examine what has been excluded from dominant discourses about the role and evolution of the body. More specifically, Tomasula leads us to reconsider the importance of our body in our reading methodologies, and to reconsider why we have repressed it from the ways in which we envision access to knowledge.

Here, my reading argues against interpretations of *VAS* that separate the enjoyment of the palpable text from the serious questions it asks. Critics underline the fascination and appeal they feel for the book, but dismiss them as diversion from the serious questions the novel asks. Vanderborg, for instance, wonders whether the "artistry," "creativity," "material messiness," and "beauty" of the novel "might distract from the violence it records" (10). I would contend that, in fact, *VAS* invites us to regard our involvement in the materiality of the novel as part of our knowledge production. Instead of separating our physical interactions with the text from its ethical questions, to approach *VAS*, we have to rethink knowledge as an embodied element. Because such rethinking implies that we reconfigure theories of knowledge, our bodily interactions with the material of the text do not distract us from the serious epistemological questions the novel considers. In other words, the writer and designer denounce the notion that cultural practices are more important and powerful than corporeal experiences.

My analysis of the bodily politics of the novel argues against Banash's interpretation of *VAS*, which claims that the novel "combines both the critical and conservative desires of collage in a single gesture" (17). Although *VAS* is critical toward the information it presents, it also uses a collage method that, essentially, aestheticizes data and provides visual pleasure for readers. The collage conserves and fetishizes old models, while performing a genealogy of these documents. While collages have been used to disrupt modes of artistic (de)figuration, for Banash they nonetheless are rooted in a conservative mode of thinking that relies on nostalgia. He adds that although collages critique social trends, they take part in the commodification of culture through their use of fragments. For Banash, therefore, the fragmentary presentation of the book also causes the commodification that *VAS* challenges: "collage mirrors or critically mobilizes the strategies of consumption by selecting ready-mades [. . . .] The technique is enmeshed in the very problems of alienation that are the commodity form itself" (27). Banash interestingly links commodities to collage, but I wish to emphasize that the participation of the reader in the collage does not take away from the politics of *VAS*. In other words, the novel's politics is not just a critique of conservative agendas, as it also allows a positive and pleasurable participation from the reader that is a political act in itself.

Such pleasurable interactions with the text rely on Tomasula's usages of "the materiality of the text: the stuff available for a writer to sculpt into the narrative" ("Narrative + Image"). In writing *VAS*, Tomasula utilized "the materiality of the text" to

> use the book as a metaphor for a body and the body as the metaphor for a book. So I think with the genetic engineering age that we're entering, that that metaphor is becoming very literal, where you're literally editing the ABCs—now the AGCTs—of DNA, and creating a type of writing that is an entity in itself, and has very, very real consequences for us and future generations. [. . .] In terms of [. . .] the body *of* the book, I was hoping that readers would start to see the body as a book by reading a book that ultimately does have a body. (personal interview)

The metaphor of the text as a body and the body as a text implies that the body, like other media, can be rewritten, modified, and edited. Here again, remediation theory is useful because it considers the refashioning of media in texts *and* bodies. Indeed, remediation theory offers tools to explore the bodies of texts, as it sets up a parallel between intermedia products and the body as a remediation material: "the surgeon first uses graphics to remediate the patient's body visually and then employs the scalpel to bring this body into agreement with the visual remediation. It is a short step from the rhetoric of natural beauty to the rhetoric of the real of the immediate" (238). Tomasula considers such remediation processes in *VAS*. Through its exploration of body modifications—the description of a surgery that *"Separate[s] carotid and subcalvian arteries of the neck and upper chest,"* among other procedures, and Cindy Jackson's eighteen plastic surgeries to "become a real-life Barbie" ([166], 260)—the novel tackles the evolution of the body as an intermedia product: mediated representations refashion the body and the book. Both have become "a *structure* to be monitored and modified" (Bolter and Grusin 240).

Hence, Tomasula not only features remediation in his use of other media, he also employs it to explore textual and bodily media. As Emily Pérez notes, "*VAS* explores issues of editing and manipulation of text as versions of editing and manipulation of the body." When reading the novel, it thus becomes necessary to examine "this interplay between the body of the text considered as a material-semiotic artifact and the bodies represented within the imaginary worlds" that *VAS* creates, or what Hayles calls "textual body" ("Bodies of Texts" 258). "Textual bodies" require that we interpret both the ways in which texts represent bodies and the ways in which these representations affect their formal mutation. As Hayles notes, an early example of "textual body" is William Burroughs's *Naked Lunch*, whose loosely connected chapters insist on the fragmentation of the textual corpus. Fissures are as much part of the book's composition as the narrative on William Lee. The junkie's body, like the fractured text, is mutated and exploded by addiction. Burroughs's exploration of a "textual body," like Tomasula's, merges form and content so that the text mimics the body and vice versa. Tomasula's work with Farrell adds a visual and tactile element to the "textual body": in approaching the novel, we metaphorically approach a body, so that our senses become central to our reading methodology.

This is evident when *VAS*'s pages and cover appear as skin. The image of the 2003 Chicago cover that opened this chapter clearly brings the book close to a body. *VAS*'s first cover, the 2002 Barrytown front cover, represents a "'Bone, Muscle, and Flesh layer' (e-mail to author, 5 July 2007), starting at the right with a cardboard section with dot-matrix style lettering in silver, bordered by a narrow vertical strip of streaked red and pink, and then a tan-pink leatherette section leading into the spine" (Vanderborg 11). In the text, we also find scars that allude to the punctures in the skin of the novel, red stains that look like the page's blood, and shifts of colors and patterns that emphasize textures. In exploring these bodily images and the content of the book about the evolution of bodies throughout time, we also explore the changes in linguistic structures, since "words [are] both the material and message of language" (58).

After elaborating on evolutionary theory, the narrator tells us, "*In fact, if you run / English's mutations in fast forward, you can watch it evolve*" (68). A text that evolves from old English to contemporary English in one paragraph follows. The paragraph playfully alludes to the comparison one can make between words and seeds, as words, like seeds, change and allow knowledge to grow even though "various censures" and the "fancies of men" affect them ([68]). Tomasula parallels the evolution of language with the evolution of the body and the ways in which we conceptualize and modify the latter to reveal that "men and mutations [. . . are] / as inseparable as seed and cell" ([68]). Hence, *VAS* invites us to understand body and textual modifications as a joint issue, which requires that we use our senses in our interpretive process. While it is clear that remediation calls for this sensual mode of reading, sensuality remains unaccounted for in Bolter and Grusin's theory. In focusing on the technical aspects of immediacy and hypermediacy, remediation theory isolates the bodily involvement it calls for. In other words, remediation clarifies the workings of intermedia modes of expression, but it does not elaborate on the sensual reading and knowing practices that originate from the reciprocal structures of remediation, which I will analyze at length in this chapter.

It is interesting to note, however, that the alternation between a sense of immediacy and hypermediacy is similar to the movement from a subject to subjectless positions in Kristeva's, Bataille's, and Barthes's theories. The vacillation between awareness of the media and immersion in it is comparable to the erotic mechanism. In that sense, *VAS*, much like *Plus, AVA,* and *DICTEE,* sets up an erotic process through a shift of subject positions. In *VAS*, this occurs through the collage of various media that causes remediation and leads to sensual reading because, as Shelley Jackson notes, in a collage method, "writing is stripped of the pretense of originality, and appears as a practice of mediation, of selection and contextualization, a practice, almost, of reading. In which one can be surprised by what one has to say, in the forced intercourse between texts or the recombinant potential in one text" [*sic*] (Jackson qtd. in Olsen "Notes"). Jackson's erotic metaphor illuminates the erotics of reading in *VAS*. Indeed, the coming in and out of fragments of texts necessitates an immersion in the textual media, which stresses the importance of our bodies as interpretive tools. During this interpretive process, we realize that "by appropriating and quoting out of context, the form releases new and often unexpected contexts, recontextualizations that can surprise the author as well as the reader" (Olsen). For Lance Olsen, such recontextualizations "draw attention to the sensuality of the page, the physicality of the book, and therefore dra[w] attention to writing as a postbiological body of text." In that sense a book like *VAS*, which highlights its materiality, calls for our own physical engagement with the textual body: "THE STUFF IN THE NEW **SYNTAX**" of *VAS* "STIMULAT[ES] FRICTION, NOW IN THE FLESH, THEN TO THE RETINA, HERE ON THE

PAGE, AS THE EYE MASSAGES THE WEARY BRAIN INTO A NEW CON-FIGURATION" (Drucker, *Figuring* 145). Hence, the scholarship on *VAS* needs more contribution on the relationship between spatiality and touch and reading and writing: How does the form of *VAS* shape, or even sculpt, our reading? Do the visual designs and print modifications call for a different reading, one that might not necessarily be available in the verbal content of the novel? How are our bodies implicated in this reading? What forms of knowledge emerge from such embodied reading methodology?

Marks's examination of haptic visuality provides a theoretical framework to answer those questions. In film, haptic images involve a gradual figuration, detailed vision, change in focus, graininess, and under- and overexposure so that "the viewer perceives the texture as much as the object imaged" (Marks *Skin* 163). The sensual look that haptic vision requires produces erotic experiences: "regardless of their content, haptic images are erotic in that they construct an intersubjective relationship between beholder and image" (Marks *Skin* 138). Building on Marks's theory, I wish to underline that, in *VAS*, this erotic mode is also part of a positive political process. *VAS*'s tactile aesthetics is not merely a formal experiment and does not only provoke abstract reconsiderations of social frameworks. In fact, it stimulates reading and representational modalities based on reciprocity.

This erotic/political mode of reading relies on the haptic's power to connect the viewer and the image. Indeed, in using remediation, Tomasula puts divergent forms together and calls attention to their intermedia activity. In doing so, he creates gaps that foster new interpretive strategies, and the reader/viewer is "called upon to fill in the gaps in the image, to engage with the traces the image leaves. By interacting up close with an image, close enough that figure and ground commingle, the viewer relinquishes her own sense of separateness from the image—not to know it, but to give herself up to her desire for it" (Marks *Skin* 183). *VAS* fosters haptic vision, which brings the reader close to the medium of the text, as Marks describes it, but the novel does not rely strictly on the haptic, as it narrates and represents Square's story. In fact, as Marks notes, when focusing on haptic visions, "the point is not to utterly replace symbolization, a form of representation that requires distance [. . . .] Rather it is to maintain a robust flow between sensuous closeness and symbolic distance" (*Touch* xiii). *VAS*'s representations rely on optical vision, but the flow between the haptic and the optical propels erotic experiences, thereby inviting the reader to revisit cultural models from a sensuous point of view.

As Rebecca Scherr indicates, "intermedial collision opens spaces for asking questions, for exploring formal strategies; it invites the audience to investigate the points of collision, to examine the work's jagged edges, and to experience the (possible) discomfort and/or pleasure elicited by such surprising juxtaposition" (146). In experiencing such "discomfort and/or pleasure," the reader is never allowed to adopt a detached position from the text. Instead, he or she is constantly drawn into the signifying process. In that sense, *VAS* points out the power dynamics that dominate and control the body, but it also asks the reader to participate in a reciprocal relationship with the textual body in which domination is not the primary factor. Consequently, *VAS* allows us to practice a mode of creation that entangles the subject and the text. On page 177, the few U.S. stamps appearing in several earlier pages accumulate excessively so that the text becomes difficult to read (see figure 24). The musical charts—they are the margin-lines around which the text is organized—that appear throughout the book also provide additional notes, distracting even more from the narrative to their left. This visual experience allows the reader to take pleasure in the arrangement of the information on the page while it also reminds readers of the political impact of this arrangement. The U.S. stamps and music elements point to blanks, alluding to the holes in any knowledge. The blanks on the page also ironically mock the need to control and own through the use of scientific and governmental patents. The blanks allude to the impossibility of simplifying our relationship with knowledge and science through ownership. Therefore, the futility of such human habits becomes obvious. This meaningless activity also comments on Square's collection of information on eugenics and body modifications and on our attempt to combine bits of information to make sense of the novel. Even though the book traces a history of body modifications and eugenics, any understanding of it will be imperfect because it is based on fragments of information. These fragments do not always connect, because there are gaps in our understanding of past or present situations. Thus, the enjoyable visual experience also enacts a political realization about knowledge in scientific or historical reports.

The text's performance of its content accentuates such erotic/political practices. Our physical relationship to the spatial arrangement of the page allows for a different way to relate to thoughts and language: on page [98], the visual presentation of the book enacts its message. Page [98] ends with the words "By delet—" and is followed by three blank pages. Then, the sentence "sometimes silence is most eloquent" appears. The reader comes close to the medium of the book, allowing the pagination to become expressive. At this moment, the reader releases control over the progression of the narrative, and the materiality of the text tells the story. This mode of reading challenges the reader's power over the text since it "implies making oneself

Nor would any Cro-Mag want Neanderthals for
their primitive organs, he reasoned. Off-the-shelf
    Cro-Mag organs were as common as widgets
grown from embryo stem cells on vast bio-farms
    for those still willing to undergo the brutal
anachronism that was surgery. He believed, as
    Cro-Mag chiefs said, that the murders were
    isolated acts of bigotry, for the truth was that
Neanderthals like himself didn't even have to stay
    Neanderthal. At least not totally. Everyone who
    had the money (which is to say everyone who mattered)
        could direct their own personal evolution
Incorporating the genes of a different species into
    your own had been protected as a form of free
speech. Having someone scrape cells from your
body in order to sell them or carry out their own
genetic project was prohibited by copyright laws
    (if a person had had the foresight to copyright themselves).
If they could get the money together (dollars still the
    hardest subject to clone) or, more commonly, if they
        had good health insurance and if the need
        arose—through illness or accident—often they
        would receive some treatment that would make
them at least partially Cro-Mag. Only Neanderthal
    fanatics, the ones who spent their days stacking
    stones into mysterious mounds, refused outright.

FIGURE 24. Steve Tomasula. *VAS: An Opera in Flatland* p. 177 (c) 2004 Steve Tomasula. The University of Chicago Press.

vulnerable to the image, reversing the relation of mastery that characterizes optical viewing" (Marks *Skin* 185). Through a play with the reader's expectations, Tomasula reverses this "relationship of mastery" when we encounter information about the "first cyborg, a lab rat fitted with a tiny / pump that injected a continuous flow of / chemicals" (145). A footnote presenting a picture of the rat reads, "Now maybe I've got your attention" (145). Here, the referent of "I" remains unclear, as it could refer to Tomasula, Square, the book, or the rat. This ambiguity plays with our expectations and calls our attention to the constructed-ness of the narrative.

In addition, the image of a rat erupting in the midst of technical information about cyborgs is unexpected, and the only image after two pages comparatively full of writing. The playful comment also ironically refers to our surprise when encountering a rat wearing a pump. Consequently, instead of merely processing the information on cyborgs, we are forced to stop and look at the image. Once again, we are invited to release control over the information and to pay attention to the medium of the book. The rat picture is itself inscribed in a book, which shows a *mise-en-abyme* of information and asks that we consider the interrelations between textual media through the presentation of a book within a book. Furthermore, if one does not look closely at the rat, the pump may appear to be a strange tail. This defective or deceptive appearance relates to the inaccessibility of images and concepts in the novel.

In that sense, *VAS*, "a Foucauldian genealogy of race, sex, and culture [. . .] [gives attention to], as Foucault would say, 'the errors, false appraisals, and the faulty calculations' (365)" (Schneiderman). As Vanderborg proposes:

> Ultimately, this visual novel acknowledges that our physiology is always overwritten by cultural histories, but it argues that, to our chagrin and sometimes our benefit, we rarely copy those texts perfectly or even redact the same fragments. *VAS* focuses on the ambiguities, omissions, and fallacies in our conflicting definitions of human identity, records that not only expose their sources' biases but can occasionally offer more chances for a "revisionist history" of bodies and communities than their authors had ever intended. *VAS*'s notes on these imperfect texts invite us to reexamine the limits of our own revisionary agency as interpreters and transmitters of evolutionary records. (5)

Indeed, *VAS* directly challenges mainstream reading and interpretive methods which are refashioned in the novel, but it also produces a positive mode of thinking. The section of *VAS* in which Circle and Square are at the opera reveals that an investigation of what is lacking from our traditional approaches to texts will produce knowledge about the relationship between texts and readers. Vanderborg writes that, during the opera, "even an unwilling spectator like Circle, who 'stop[s] watching' the drama in 'the third act,' leaves a mark on its composition" (8). We can infer, then, that defective readings, which are as incomplete as the faulty narratives presented in the novel, may be just as revealing, if not more, than readings and narratives that claim to encompass their subject matter. The flaws of our reading methodologies are what become important; in traveling through a mass of imperfect texts, we also reassess the imperfections of our reading techniques.

VAS calls for this mode of reading in its use visual erotics: the haptic experience of the novel gives the impression of seeing the object for the first time because the haptic image "resolves into figuration only gradually, if at all" (Marks *Skin* 163). We experience this when the visual and linguistic print accumulate and bleed into one another excessively. Page 254 presents the collage of the larynx of a dead man with gray prints underneath (see figure 25).

Exploring each part of the collage carefully, we realize that there are words written in gray between the body parts, but because the gray in the picture matches the gray of the letters, we have to come close to the texture of each part of the collage to see some letters and even decipher certain words, such as "culturing" and "three." The picture is superimposed on a stamp and on other illegible texts. The accumulation of data on these pages calls for an examination of symmetrical patterns: the larynxes parallel one another even though they are different sizes, and the information at the bottom (the Kodak brand and the number of each picture) is also set up as a mirror. We cannot easily make sense of the facing page.

On page 255, the red traces that appear vertically on the right-hand side of the page remind us of blood, but could also be waves of frequency. In addition, the circles on which are printed RNA Pol II, TAFs, etc. look like medical pills or drawings of cells in a science book. The black traces around the middle gray circles resemble the triple forte below which reminds us that this installation is in fact laid out on a musical staff, itself transformed into a medical chart with a frequency from 0 to 4 kcps. Arrows and writings obscure the quote by Thomas Hobbes. Hence, the interpretation of this large amount of data remains difficult, if not impossible, and we make sense of parts of the text only gradually.

Our eye follows various visual leads, focusing on the textures and colors to make sense of the visual text. In doing so, the motion of our eye, as

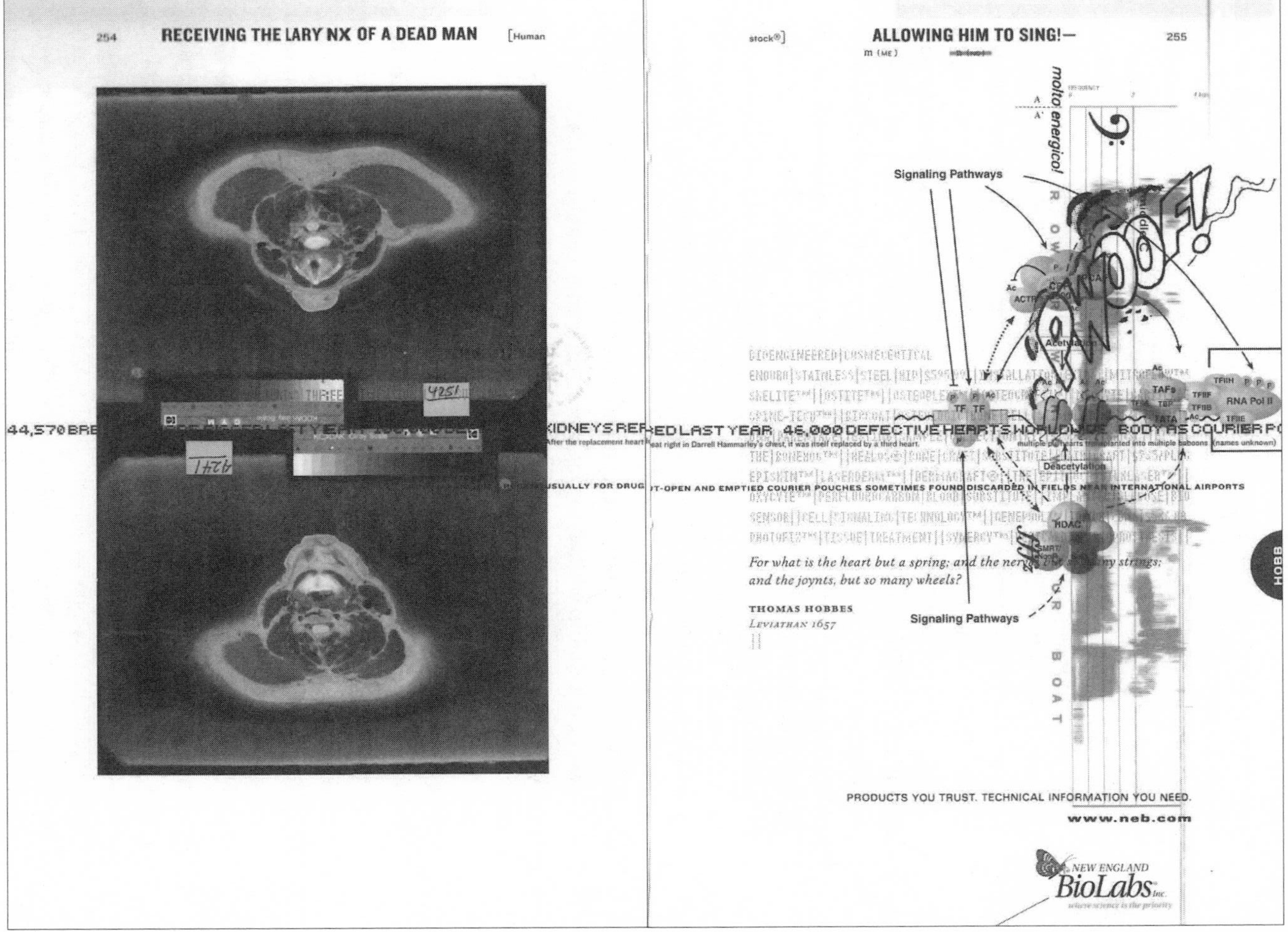

FIGURE 25. Steve Tomasula. *VAS: An Opera in Flatland* p. 254–55. (c) 2004 Steve Tomasula. The University of Chicago Press.

it focuses on the graininess of each color, compares to the hand's motion on a body. The hand and eye movements are close here, since we focus on the palpable qualities of materials. The pleasure of this exploration lies in connecting things visually, since we realize that it is impossible to decipher each part of the collage and reach a cohesive conclusion about its meaning. Consequently, our goal is not to master the image, to make sense of it and to move on to the next page. Instead, we are invited to spend time exploring the textures, colors, and spatial arrangement of the material.

In doing so, we come so close to the material of the text that we momentarily lose our sense of proportion and focus instead on the textures and grain of the text. Indeed, "Haptic images do not invite identification with a figure so much as they encourage a bodily relationship between the viewer and the image" (Marks *Touch* 3). In experiencing the "sensuous, fragmented surface, a surface that robs the viewer of perspective and orientation with respect to it," the reader's "(embodied) eye" generates "sensuous immediacy" (Bernstein 155). Thus, "it is less appropriate to speak of the object of a haptic look than to speak of a dynamic subjectivity between looker and image" (Marks *Touch* 3). Because touch does not isolate the subject from the object, it involves a mutual production of reader and text. We do not get a full understanding of the picture at first glance, but we are invited to participate in the flow of colors and textures and to accept and enjoy the ambiguity of its signification. This enjoyment involves a gradual figuration of the media that Tomasula implicitly compares to the gradual and fragmentary understanding of ideologies: through a reading that cannot reach a coherent understanding of the accumulated data, we are performing the mode of thinking that the medium calls for.

This sensual/political mode of reading is best understood in parallel with Oval's scientific experiments. Because Tomasula includes Oval's scientific activities in the novel, we end up trying to solve them, just like her. It is no coincidence that our reading process is comparable to Oval's experiments, rather than to her learning science through a lecture or a textbook. In fact, our pleasure in reading corresponds to Oval's excitement in the physical experience of playing with pieces of scientific puzzles. Like her, through touching and feeling objects, we discern how different models shape our thought processes. Tomasula transfers this tactile and playful method to our reading experience, which in turn exposes and challenges the constricting nature of dominant reading and knowledge models, thereby revealing their fragility. Because we participate in the signifying process of *VAS*'s collage, we also realize that such models can be disrupted. Here, "the critic who approaches the text erotically [. . .] is a producer and cocreator of textuality, not a consumer who exists independent of the text" (Ott "Television" 306). Thus, the mutual constitution of subject and text allows alternative ways to interact with literary and social texts. In that sense, "the sensory experience" of the reading of *VAS* "is not the simple filling out of an antecedent structure, but formative" (Bernstein 3).

This formative reading occurs when, for example, *VAS* presents a playful and cartoon-like exercise on perception that is part of Oval's science kit (see figure 26):

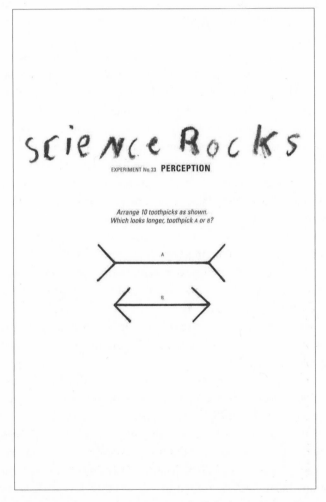

FIGURE 26. Steve Tomasula. *VAS: An Opera in Flatland* p. 50 (c) 2004 Steve Tomasula. The University of Chicago Press.

In the example, although A and B are the same length, A appears longer, revealing that our perceptions may differ depending on the arrangement of information. This exercise closely relates to our experience of the two serious quotes appearing on page [96]: "*'The rapid growth of the feeble-minded classes coupled as it is with / steady reduction among all superior stocks constitutes a race danger / which should be cut off before another year has passed.'*—WINSTON CHURCHILL." On the opposite page, we read: "*'Whoever is not bodily and spiritually healthy and worthy shall not / have the right to pass on his suffering in the body of his children.'*—ADOLF HITLER" (97). The juxtaposition of the quotes reveals that the political agendas of leaders we would never associate were actually closer than we think. Indeed,

> One of the ideas that circulates through *VAS* is the way that we demonize Hitler all the time, and rightfully so, but the danger in demonizing Hitler is to not recognize how natural it was for him to put the extermination of undesirables into play. The novel asks us to remember that Germany was only the eleventh industrialized nation to legalize the elimination of "undesirables"—it took twenty years before the Nazis got around to it. Winston Churchill, the government here in the U.S.—they were all saying the same kinds of basic things until Hitler took it to its extreme, but logical, conclusion. (personal interview)

Hence, depending on the context in which one presents these two leaders, one may understand their political goals differently. The perception exercise and the juxtaposition of Hitler's words and Churchill's declaration reveal that any data is constructed; it is a part of the biases of its time and place. These conclusions also apply to the novel itself, since *VAS* combines information so that we become aware of the manipulation at stake in the construction of *any* knowledge.

In addition, in the passages cited above, the body is a site of social control and domination. The acceptable body reproduces the prevailing norms, while the "unhealthy" and "inferior body" is banished. We realize that Churchill and Hitler shared surprisingly similar viewpoints, but we also realize that we reach this conclusion thanks to *VAS*'s pre-set parameters, just like Oval's "home experiments" (26). Because *VAS* points to the inaccuracies and limits of any narrative, we are led to ask whether *VAS* itself is complicit in the discourses of new reproduction technologies and body modifications it is presenting. This double awareness—about the social myths we have taken for granted and about the manipulative choices of the book's arrangement itself—reveals that all texts are incomplete and marked by social biases.

By participating in the incompleteness of *VAS*, however, we also realize that the mutual constitution of subject and text allows alternative ways to interact with literary and social texts. In sum, on the one hand, *VAS* shows that the body, like the text, has become a political locus that reflects scientific, ideological, and political tensions. In that sense, the novel confirms that the body is a discursive site that can be read and interpreted like other cultural products. On the other hand, *VAS* does not consider the body strictly as a discursive formation because, in engaging our bodies in the signifying process of the novel, we allow them to participate in cultural shapings. In other words, *VAS* leads us to consider the cultural molds that affect the body, but it also insists on the body's intervening possibilities. While the body is a social product, it also has the ability to participate in cultural productions.

For Tomasula, this participation is established through the double-helix structuring principle of the novel. This structuring clarifies the possibilities of the dual role of the body as a political agent and object. As I will explain, the double-helix structure penetrates the book on different levels—the space of the book, its language, and the role of the reader's body. First, the double-helix organization is spatial, not thematic. On page [57] different frameworks and typefaces are mixed: the typeface used to convey the narrative mingles with the typeface used to transcribe chromosome 12 later in the book. The mixing of the DNA typeface and the typeface used to tell the story alludes to the organizing pattern in the book, which follows a double-helix organizing principle. AGCTs that split to form a genetic pattern constitute the DNA ladder. This pattern is congruent with the writing of *VAS*, in which information gathers similarly. In this sense, the book and the body work as a double helix. Square points out these parallels between body and text, emphasizing the importance of the DNA, "written in a language of / four base letters, *AGCT,* which combined into / words—*CAG/ATA/AGG*—the words forming / double-helix sentences of genes which filled / pages of chromosomes within the cells which / made up the book of his body" (51). In addition, the musical lines mimicking a musical score resemble the double-helix configuration of the DNA since, on them, ideas will come to assemble "harmonies, sometimes discords, or sometimes forming mutations, sometimes proteins" (Tomasula, personal correspondence).

Second, language itself has undergone modifications much like the mutations of DNA in *VAS*:

To undercut the idea of a completed book "fixed in print" in its "final draft" (56), there are playful small "typos" and "pun[s]" (67, 304) on other pages, e.g., the substitution of *"loose"* for *"lose"* in a passage about mistakes in genetic copying (307), the phrase "a metaphor for it's time" (304), or the reference about sexual coupling in the biblical "DEUTERONOMY" (66). (Vanderborg 9)

As Vanderborg notes, some of these misspellings occurred because of "communication problems with the printer in China," but the author came to accept these occurrences "in the spirit of mutation" (Tomasula qtd. in Vanderborg 11). In this spirit, Tomasula "introduc[ed] some typos" into "the stretch of genetic code" for chromosome 12 in order "to reverse evolve human [code] closer to [that of] the chimp" (Vanderborg 11). This erroneous writing of the chromosome code, which appears on pages [202] through [227] and which also emerges on other pages of the book (including its cover page), is re-utilized at the end of the novel, in the opera. In this case, the chromosome code is not just presented as part of a collage: the typeface used to write it is the same used to write the text of cartoons. In addition, it does not appear as an interruption of the text, which is usually the case in the rest of the novel. This time, the code is part of the lyrics of the opera Square watches with his wife. Here, the code is not just an abstraction of the body: through the voice of the singer, the chromosome becomes part of the singer's body. This transformation of the role of the chromosome code follows the modification pattern of the book: bodies rely on chromosomes, and at the end of the novel, after the evolution of the text, the chromosome also relies on a voice to be expressed. The change in typefaces in the transcription of the code reinforces the modification process of the book. While the author insists on the mutations that affect bodily and literary texts here, he also designs *VAS* so that we are forced to engage in the modification process. Thus, the reader takes part in the double-helix activity when engaging with the textual body.

This third aspect of the double-helix principle is exemplified on pages [21–22] (see figure 27): This is a picture of a book with tabs, which looks like a dictionary or encyclopedia or *VAS*. The representation of a book within a book evokes the metafictional experiments of Madeline Gins in *Word Rain,* where she inserts a picture of the book on the title page. The self-referentiality of the picture is in line with the book's content, which invites readers to look at the words, at the sentences, at the book. In the context of *VAS,* pages [21–22] encourage us, in turning the page, to connect the sexuality of the apes as defined by Desmond Morris to the map of human sexuality illustrated in the next page by a naked male and female body facing one another so that they "perform" intercourse as we turn the page. This activity illustrates the comment at the bottom of the page that

For pair bonding and therefore civilization to develop, the naked ape had to acquire a capacity to become sexually imprinted on a single partner. It did so by linking sex to identity through evolutionary changes that favored face-to-face copulation....Copulation is most commonly performed with the naked male over the naked female, with the female's legs apart.

DESMOND MORRIS
The Naked Ape, 1967

FIGURE 27. Steve Tomasula. *VAS: An Opera in Flatland* p. 21 (c) 2004 Steve Tomasula. The University of Chicago Press.

"the partner's genitals may also / become the target for repeated actions. Often rhythmically" ([23]).

The information resembles a biology book, a mode of presentation reminiscent of illustrations found in earlier novels, such as Kurt Vonnegut's *Breakfast of Champions* and its famous drawings of an "asshole," ice cream cone, underwear, bombs, and so forth. Vonnegut's pictures appear as illustrations in a children's book to explain simple concepts, so that, like *VAS*'s pages [21–22], they make us smile. As adults, the visual presentation of commonplace objects or basic actions is humorous because images are not necessary to our understanding. Yet, in Vonnegut's novel, many of these images represent serious human matters—war and sex, for instance. Similarly, in *VAS*, the playful representation of human sexuality has serious consequences: it does not, like Vonnegut's drawings, illustrate the content of the narrative, but it forces us to perform it through our reading act. This erotic act enacted through the reading process reinforces the erotic capabilities of reading. Hence, through his or her reading, the reader adopts different modes of data organization, trying them out while understanding their limits and constructed-ness. In touching the medium of the text, the reader changes the text as well as him- or herself.

Consequently, characterizing *VAS* as a critique of dominant models, as readers of formally innovative fiction tend to do, is not wrong, but it does not do justice to the embodied methodology it produces. What is particularly interesting about Tomasula's work is that we question the ways in which the body has been understood and presented throughout time because we *experience* a mode of thinking that does not divorce body and thought. *VAS* invites us to participate in the creation of meaning in the text so that reader and text are continually absorbed in a process of mutual constitution. In other words, we come to practice the rethinking *VAS* provokes because the novel foregrounds sensual interactions between reader and text. These interactions rely on a movement in and out of the medium of the text that combines erotics and politics. Indeed, this immersion in the story and the reflection on the constructed-ness of information engages an erotic movement in and out of the control of oneself. Through this process, Tomasula reveals the political stakes of an erotics of reading: the novel calls for a kind of political activism that differs from conventional definitions and that does not merely resist traditional modes of writing and thinking. In *VAS*, one does not rely on following a guiding voice that tells one what to do or how to resist grand narratives, propaganda, or the manipulation of knowledge. Consequently, Tomasula locates political changes within the erotic realm, thereby imagining routes out of traditional political engagement.

c o n c l u s i o n

      Traditionally, critics think that experimental fictions, in their disruption of conventional storytelling and language uses, propose a counterpractice that resists literary and social customs. The attention given to these fictions' resistance has been and remains vital to the reading of innovative works, but, as the preceding chapters have shown, this interpretation fails to register the positive experience of aesthetic recovery recorded by practitioners and partisans of recent innovative fiction. In proposing an interpretive apparatus to examine the sensual experience of readers in their engagement with the language and material of fiction, this project has offered a counterview to the emphasis on the strictly privative character of formally innovative novels. Thus, an erotics of reading clarifies the interrelations between reader and text according to new models of language as sensual engagement. Considering senses and emotions as critical interpretive tools implies that the artistic act is mutually constitutive: *Plus, AVA, DICTEE,* and *VAS* invite an embodied approach to reading during which we construct the text while also constructing ourselves. This positive relation to experience reconfigures reading methods, producing a physical relationship to texts.

While these novels' exploration and engagement of the body comprise rich case studies to examine blissful reading practices, they are not isolated cases. Other contemporary works call for readers' interaction with linguistic and textual materiality and foster a reconsideration of the relationship between body and text. Ben Marcus's *The Age of Wire and String* (1995) invites readers to decode a grammar of bodily actions—pain, instinct, and emotion. Markson's *Reader's Block* (1996) offers a narrative that is "Non-linear. Discontinuous. Collage-like. An assemblage," that is "[o]bstinately cross-referential and of cryptic interconnective syntax in any case" (193, 140). Markson's paratactic sentences flirt with the white space separating them, taking us on a fluid journey about writers' deaths and tragic fates. In Thalia Field's *POINT AND LINE* (2000), the narrative takes the form of composite discourses exploring thought, language, and the body. The result is a sensual exploration of "the touch [that] might be painful, erotic, before we understand it" (9), and of "the body [which] is the blueprint of all technology" (25). Lidia Yuknavitch's *Real to Reel* (2003) explores bodily realities through metaphors of cinematography: "I picture you in scenes of longing so great my brain nearly explodes inside the shell of its skull" (63); "If he could produce a picture he would produce one of the human body lost to death but living like words. A frozen image" (119); "Broken into white, black lifeless twigs moving in obscene jerking tilts. Arms retrieve sticks from fallen trees. Legs barely able to carry a body pushing through blankets of white as if slow motion or a broken film. As if the entire photo were overexposed, the humans faint impressions of themselves" (121). Leslie Scalapino notes in her foreword to *Dahlia's Iris—Secret Autobiography + Fiction* (2003) that her novel "is divided between perceiving and actions in a space—[she is] trying to bring these together on one space (throughout), where thinking and one's sensations would be (are) actions there too" (v). The book explores the impossibilities of the corporeal experience of perceiving and acting, as well as interiority and exteriority in a syntax as paradoxical as these explorations. The "Contributor's Notes" of Michael Martone's *Michael Martone* (2005) call attention to the texts we often overlook in novels: in playing with the form of the contributor's note, Martone points out the materiality of his book—what constructs it and frames it in a writing tradition. For Martone, the writerly constraints that shape such notes are parallel to the constructions of the various Michael Martones. Michael Joyce's *Was* (2007) explores the fleetingness of information through vivid fragments of life that take the form of complete and incomplete sentences whisking across pages to construct a nomadic narrative. In the first few pages of Everett's *The Water Cure* (2007), we read:

> Fragments. Frag-ments. Frags. Fr. m ents. This work is not fragmented;
> it is fragments. (16)

The non sequitur fragments relate the murder of the narrator's daughter, whose body, like the narrative, was cut into pieces. In his quest to avenge his daughter, the protagonist tortures the killer, so that bodily and narrative abrasions coincide. Olsen's *Head in Flames* (2009) is "a collage text composed of chips of sensation, observation, memory, and quotation shaped into a series of narraticules told by three alternating voices, each inhabiting a different font and aesthetic/political/existential space" (Olsen *Rampike* 56). The fragments, typefaces, and white spaces manifest the correlation between art, passion, and politics. The fictions of Markson, Field, Yuknavitch, Scalapino, Martone, Joyce, Everett, and Olsen provide examples of erotic modes of writing that enable the construction of an intersubjective relationship between reader and text, while also revealing the social and political customs that shape narratives and self-representations.

The erotic politics of these texts brings into question their form and content, as well as their appearance and frameworks, which prefigures the kinds of engagements that New Media texts call for in their dynamic fusion of the body and textual/material. As Christiane Paul notes, in the digital medium we are "confronted with complex possibilities" of "the user's or participant's involvement" in "remote and immediate intervention" (67). While these interventions are the basis of the digital medium, they are foreshadowed in the novels of McElroy, Maso, Cha, and Tomasula. Thus, it will come as no surprise that some of the authors listed above have also explored digital literature and New Media. Joyce's hypertext fiction *Twelve Blue* (1996) includes interactive threads of narrative, that "like sensual lovemaking [. . .] tak[e] time to develop and cannot be rushed" (Hayles *Electronic Literature* 64). Olsen's hypermedia novel *10:01* (2005) offers a fragmented account of movie-going in America—its historical correlation with capitalism, commodification, individualism, and identity construction. Tomasula's New Media novel *TOC* (2009) presents an assemblage of text, film, music, photography, spoken words, animation, and painting about our conception and experience of time. *Twelve Blue, 10:01, TOC,* and other New Media works, including Jackson's *Patchwork Girl* (1995), Laurie Anderson's *Puppet Motel* (1995), Mark Amerika's *GRAMMATRON* (1997), and Tal Halpern's *Digital Nature* (2002), point out and utilize the convergence between body and text. The reader weaves through Jackson's visual illustrations and textual explorations of female body parts stitched together. Upon launching Anderson's CD-ROM, the user hears a voice warning, "You are out of memory. Save. Save now." The compilation of monologues, videos, and visual texts that follows is haunted by puppets, who, lost in a "motel" of technical devices (clocks, flashlights, answering machines, telephones, TVs, etc.), ask to be loved or remembered. In *GRAMMATRON*, readers click on words while watching digitally animated images retelling the Golem myth and exploring the new language that grows out of technological advancements and New Media creations. Halpern's *Digital Nature* takes us through "The Case Collection," composed of rescued narratives that remediate old artifacts ("Travelogues, colonial photographs, and naturalist's maps") into interactive links, so that the reader "explore[s] how different media forms interact to produce a broader field of perceptual possibilities delimiting what can be said and seen within a given historical moment" (Halpern "Shots"). In these works, bodily and conceptual interpretive processes interrelate with the materiality of fiction. The mediation of the body relies on the kinds of corporeal readings and perceptions explored in *Plus, AVA, DICTEE,* and *VAS,* but they also include physical interactions with the machine and media when generating meaning.

These interactions add a layer of textual erotics: embodied processes are the enablers of textual production. Thus, as Hayles point out, in the digital realm, materiality takes on another meaning: it involves not only the "interactions between physical properties and a work's artistic strategies" but also "the user's interactions with the work" (*Writing Machine* 32). This does not imply that works lose the materiality of the word elaborated in Drucker's work, but in New Media texts, typography is "rethought, reconfigured": materiality changes with the advancement of New Media, but is not eliminated (Drucker "Synthetic Sensibilities"). As Matthew Kirschenbaum notes, the physical properties of New Media include their forensic existence, so that writing frameworks and mechanisms, as well as their storage, are part of our relationship with them (9–14).

This view of New Media's material existence resists claims of digital texts' ephemerality and disembodiment. While the interrelation of machine and viewer/reader has often been regarded as abstracting or immaterializing, the engagement of the body in the fictions of Tomasula, Joyce, Olsen, Halpern, Amerika, and Anderson reveals that visceral bodily activities shape meaning. For Hayles, such involvement of the body in the text is a mode of "intermediation," or that which concerns the "complex transactions between bodies and texts as well as between different forms of media" (*My*

Mother 7). Intermediation merges technological functions with the embodied human world so that texts cannot be immaterial; they are "invested with the nuanced senses of their materialities," and the "physical characteristics, verbal content, and nonverbal signifying strategies work together to produce the object called 'text'" (Hayles *My Mother* 105). Hansen's work on the body's perceptual and cognitive processes clarifies such embodied activity: in New Media, "the 'image' has itself become a process and, as such, has become irreducibly bound up with the activity of the body" (10). This implies that the image is not merely the result of technological advancements, but that it "demarcates the very process through which the body, in conjunction with the various apparatuses for rendering information perceptible, gives form to or *in-forms* information" (10). For example, in James Coleman's *Box,* Hansen notes, the repetition of flashes of a boxing match converts the boxing rhythms into the rhythms of the pulsing body of the viewer (29). For Hansen, this conversion is haptic, as it suggests that "*we 'see' with our bodies*" (110). This understanding of the "*digital image*" and the haptic implies that the development of New Media literature grew not only from the advancement of technological possibilities but also from the embodied research of literary texts and theories that have anticipated the "*displacement of the framing function of medial interfaces back onto the body from which they themselves originally sprang*" (Hansen 10, 22).

Explorations of haptic visuality and embodied responses are foregrounded in New Media fictions, as well as in art installations and experiments that consider the body as the site for meaning-making and for the artistic process. Camille Utterback's *Text Rain* (1999) is an "interactive installation in which participants use the familiar instrument of their bodies, to do what seems magical—to lift and play with falling letters that do not really exist." The installation engages the participants' bodies as they stand or move in front of a large projection screen, on which is projected an image of themselves, combined with a color animation of falling letters that react to their motions. "The falling text will 'land' on anything darker than a certain threshold, and 'fall' whenever that obstacle is removed," so that users literally construct the text through their movements. Here, the artwork does not have complete autonomy: its actualization relies on the body's activity. Another example is Graham Harwood's "Rehearsal of Memory" (1995), an interactive program "embodying the life experience of those involved" by creating "an anonymous computer personality made up of the collective experience of [a] group" of inmates (Harwood). The viewer is invited to uncover fragments of texts transposed over body parts, blending the body with the psychological accounts of serial killers, rapists, or potential suicides. Harwood invites the body in the signifying process about the casualties of the excesses of society that we are inclined to forget. Finally, Eduardo Kac's exploration of real-time dialogic exchanges between bodies and machines exemplifies art's dependence on the activity of the body. In his 1997 biobotic work, "A-positive," a human body and "a robot have direct physical contact via an intravenous needle connected to clear tubing and feed one another in a mutually nourishing relationship" ("Art"). The "bio-bot" uses red blood cells to function, creating a symbiotic exchange. The divide between the virtual and the physical no longer exists, so that the body literally hosts the artistic endeavor. These configurations of bodies and texts result in the creation of what Hayles calls the "posthuman," or that which seamlessly articulates machines and humans. This articulation implies that there is no demarcation between the technological and the bodily, so that, as in the works of Utterback, Harwood, and Kac, art is created by a fusion of body and machine.

This emphasis on bodily experiences in New Media implies that the considerations of Bataille, Kristeva, Barthes, Lecercle, Deleuze, Guattari, and Cixous on the political, ethical, and sexual significance of the synthesis of language and the subject also inform the development of New Media studies. It has been more traditional to underline New Media and post-structural theories' common concern for "the instability and intertextuality of the text, the loss of authority of the author, and the changed relationship between author, text, and reader" (Bolter 19). Yet, the research on the sensuality of the textual medium remains largely unexplored in connection to New Media studies. It is revealing for the history of New Media studies and studies of erotics that accounts of virtual reality, cyber literature, and digital media explore the relationship between viewer and textual media in terms that echo those associated with the erotic subject. Nell Tenhaaf stresses that "the widespread fascination with virtual reality technologies attests to [. . .] the wish to experience a perceptual event so immediate that it eliminates the self who must ascribe meaning to it" (57). She adds that

> This is a condition of technological symbiosis, the psyche penetrated so that the self leaks out and the not-self flows in. Subjectivity has an altered meaning and representation seems to be suspended, because there is a collapse of the familiar paradigm in which self is distinct from other, and subject "reads" object. (57)

Tenhaaf's analysis of the self in contact with virtual reality is reminiscent of the treatment of the erotic self in the works of Bataille, Barthes, Kristeva,

Cixous, and Lecercle. New Media works challenge accepted "notions of the body, not only as a culturally constructed notion and text but also as lived experience and material form," much like in books such as *Plus, AVA, DICTEE,* and *VAS* (Gromala and Sharir 281). Their common concern for a reevaluation of the body through an erotic connection with the materials of texts reframes the history of theories of eroticism and New Media studies.

Stressing the link between New Media studies and erotics not only reshapes our understanding of eroticism but also enables new perspectives in the field of New Media studies. As Bolter reveals, "Hypertext theory was [...] identified with formalist theory [....] Hypertext fictions themselves certainly looked like formalist exercises," and "hypertext theory also seemed to be associated with technological determinism," implying "that technologies could work as autonomous agents of social change" (19). To envisage theories of desire and erotics as the antecedents of New Media allows us to untie them from the obsolete body of formal critical theory and the narrowness of technological determinism. Thinking of New Media studies in this way will permit further discussion of New Media through its shared interest with theories of the erotic.

works cited

Abbott, Edwin A. *Flatland: A Romance of Many Dimensions*. New York: Dover, 1992. Print.

Abrioux, Yves. "Vectoral Muscle in a Great Field of Process: Approaching the Dynamics of *Women and Men*." *Sources* 11 (2001): 38–54. Print.

Alexander, Jacqui. *Pedagogies of Crossing: Meditations on Feminism, Sexual Politics, Memory, and The Sacred*. Durham and London: Duke UP, 2005. Print.

Amerika, Mark. *GRAMMATRON*. 1997. Web. 4 April 2011.

Amireh, Amal, and Lisa Suhair Majaj. *Going Global: The Transnational Reception of Third World Women Writers*. New York: Routledge, 2000. Print.

Anderson, Laurie. *Puppet Motel*. The Voyager Company, 1995. CD-ROM.

Banash, David. "Irrational Killers and Collecting Detectives: Critique, Nostalgia, and the Dialectics of Collage." 2005. TS. David Banash, Western Illinois University.

Banting, Pamela. "The Body as Pictogram: Rethinking Hélène Cixous's *écriture féminine*." *Textual Practice* 6.2 (1992): 225–46. Print.

Barth, John. *Lost in the Funhouse*. New York: Anchor Books, 1988. Print.

Barthes, Roland. *Camera Lucida*. Trans. Richard Howard. New York: Hill and Wang, 1981. Print.

———. *A Lover's Discourse: Fragments*. Trans. Richard Howard. New York: Hill and Wang, 1978. Print.

———. *The Pleasure of the Text*. Trans. Richard Miller. New York: Hill and Wang, 1975. Print.

———. *S/Z*. Trans. Richard Howard. New York: Hill and Wang, 1975. Print.

Bataille, Georges. *Eroticism*. Trans. Mary Dalwood. London and New York: Marion Boyars, 1987. Print.

Benthien, Claudia. Trans. Thomas Dunlap. *Skin: On the Cultural Border Between Self and the World*. New York: Columbia UP, 2002. Print.

Berila, Elizabeth. "The Art of Change: Experimental Writing, Cultural Activism, and Feminist Social Transformation." Diss. Syracuse University, 2002. Ann Arbor: UMI, 2002. ATT 3076830. Print.

Berlin, Monica. "Approaches to Carole Maso's *AVA*." *AVA* CASEBOOK. n.d. Web. 19 August 2007.

Bernstein, J. M. *Voluptuous Bodies*. Stanford: Stanford UP, 2006. Print.

Berry, R. M. "The Avant Garde and the Question of Literature." *Soundings: A Journal of Interdisciplinary Study* 88.1–2 (2005): 105–27. Print.

Bolter, Jay David. "Theory and Practice of New Media Studies." *Digital Media Revisited: Theoretical and Conceptual Innovations in Digital Domains*. Gunnar Liestøl, Andrew Morrison, and Terje Rasmussen, eds. Cambridge: MIT Press, 2004. 15–34. Print.

Bolter, Jay David, and Richard Grusin. *Remediation: Understanding New Media*. Cambridge and London: MIT Press, 1999. Print.

Brooke-Rose, Christine. *A Rhetoric of the Unreal. Studies in Narrative and Structure, Especially of the Fantastic*. Cambridge: Cambridge UP, 1983. Print.

Cha, Theresa Hak Kyung. *DICTEE*. Berkley: U of California P, 2001. Print.

Chang, Juliana. "'Transform This Nothingness': Theresa Hak Kyung Cha's *Dictee*." *Critical Mass* 1.1 (1993): 75–82. Print.

———. "Word and Flesh: Materiality, Violence and Asian American Poetics." Diss. University of California at Berkeley, 1995. Ann Arbor: UMI, 1995. AAT 9602506. Print.

Chénetier, Marc. *Sgraffites, encres & sanguines*. Paris: Presses de l'ENS, 1994. Print.

Chew, Kristina Julie. Pears Bearing Apples: Virgil's 'Georgics,' Plato's 'Phaedrus,' Theresa Hak Kyung Cha's 'Dictee.'" Diss. Yale University, 1995. Ann Arbor: UMI, 1995. AAT 9537742. Print.

Choe, Anita. "A Novena of Rebirth." *Hitting Critical Mass* 3.2 (1996): 75–84. Print.

Cixous, Hélène. "Coming to Writing." Trans. Deborah Jenson. *Coming to Writing and Other Essays*. Cambridge and London: Harvard UP, 1991. 1–58. Print.

———. "The Laugh of Medusa." Trans. Keith Cohen and Paula Cohen. *Journal of Women in Culture and Society* 1.4 (1976): 875–93. Print.

———. "Sorties. Out and Out: Attacks/Way Out/Forays." Trans. Betsi Wing. *The Logic of the Gift. Toward an Ethic of Generosity*. Alain D. Schrift, ed. New York and London: Routledge, 1992. 148–73. Print.

———. *The Third Body*. Trans. Keith Cohen. Evanston, IL: Northwestern UP, 1999. Print.

———, and Mireille Calle-Gruber. *Hélène Cixous. Rootprint. Memory and Life Writing*. London and New York: Routledge, 1997. Print.

Clark, T. J. *Farewell to an Idea: Episodes from a History of Modernism*. New Haven and London: Yale UP, 1999. Print.

Cooley, Nicole. "Textual Bodies: Carole Maso's *AVA* and the Poetics of OVER REACHING." *AVA* CASEBOOK. n.d.Web. 19 August 2007.

Cornis-Pope, Marcel. *Narrative Innovation and Cultural Rewriting in the Cold War Era*. New York: Palgrave, 2001. Print.

Csorvasi, Veronica Iulia. *In Search of a New Syntax: Maxine Hong Kingston and The-*

resa Hak Kyung Cha. MA Thesis. University of Texas at Arlington, 1999. Ann Arbor: UMI, 1999. AAT 1396530. Print.

Culler, Jonathan D. "Barthes, Theorist." *The Yale Journal of Criticism* 14.2 (Fall 2001): 439–46. Print.

Daileader, Celia. *Eroticism on the Renaissance Stage: Transcendence, Desire, and the Limits of the Visible.* Cambridge: Cambridge UP, 1998. Print.

Danielewski, Mark. *House of Leaves.* New York: Pantheon Books, 2000. Print.

DeKoven, Marianne. *A Different Language: Gertrude Stein's Experimental Writing.* Madison: U of Wisconsin P, 1983. Print.

Deleuze, Gilles, and Félix Guattari. *A Thousand Plateaus: Capitalism and Schizophrenia.* Trans. Brian Massumi. Minneapolis: U of Minnesota P, 1987. Print.

Didi-Huberman, Georges. *Confronting Images: Questioning the Ends of a Certain History of Art.* Trans. John Goodman. University Park: Pennsylvania State UP, 2005. Print.

Drucker, Johanna. *The Century of Artists' Books.* New York: Granary Books, 1995. Print.

———. *Figuring the Word: Essays on Books, Writing and Visual Poetics.* New York: Granary Books, 1998. Print.

———. "Synthetic Sensibilities: New York in a Long Tradition." In *CORTEXt: A Survey of Recent Visual Poetry,* curated by Nicholas Frank and Bob Harrison, n.p. Milwaukee: Hermetic Gallery.

———. "Typographic Intelligence: The Work of Matthew Carter." *Typography Speaking: The Art of Matthew Carter.* Margaret Re, ed. New York: Princeton Architectural Press, 2003. 9–12. Print.

———. *The Visible Word: Experimental Typography and Modern Art, 1909–1923.* Chicago: U of Chicago P, 1997. Print.

Dworkin, Andrea. *Pornography: Men Possessing Women.* London: Women's Press, 1983. Print.

Eagleton, Terry. *Against the Grain: Selected Essays.* New York and London: Verso, 1986. Print.

———. *The Illusions of Postmodernism.* Cambridge: Blackwell, 1996. Print.

Ebert, Teresa L. "The 'Difference' of Postmodern Feminism." *College English* 53.8 (1991): 886–904. Print.

Eileraas, Karina. "Between Image and Identity: Fantasy, Transnational Trauma, and Feminist Misrecognition." Diss. University of California, 2003. Ann Arbor: UMI, 2003. AAT 3088985. Print.

Everett, Anna, and John T. Caldwell. *New Media: Theories and Practice of Digitextuality.* New York: Routledge, 2003. Print.

Everett, Percival. *Walk Me to the Distance.* London: Century Hutchinson Pub Group, 1986. Print.

———. *The Water Cure.* Saint Paul: Graywolf Press, 2007. Print.

Federman, Raymond. *Critifiction: Postmodern Essays.* Albany: SUNY P, 1993. Print.

———. *Double or Nothing.* Tallahassee, FL: FC2, 1999. Print.

———. *Surfiction: Fiction Now and Tomorrow.* Chicago: Swallow P, 1975. Print.

———. *Take It or Leave It.* Normal, IL: FC2, 1997. Print.

Féral, Josette. "Antigone or the Irony of the Tribe." *Diacritics* 8.3 (1978): 2–14. Print.

Field, Thalia. *POINT AND LINE*. New York: New Directions, 2000. Print.

Flake, Emily. Review of *VAS*. *Baltimore City Paper*. 2 Feb. 2005. Web. 28 March 2008.

Fleisher, Kass. "Word Made Flesh and Blood." *American Book Review* 25.2 (2004): 3–4. Print.

Fuery, Patrick, *Theories of Desire*. Melbourne: Melbourne UP, 1995. Print.

Gass, William. *Willie Masters' Lonesome Wife*. Normal, IL: Dalkey Archive Press, 1992. Print.

Getsi Cordell, Lucia. "The Desire of Song to Be an Ear: *AVA* and the Reformation of Genre." *AVA* CASEBOOK. n.d.Web. 19 August 2007.

Gibbons, Luke. "Narratives of No Return: James Coleman's guaiRE." *James Coleman*. George Baker, ed. Cambridge and London: MIT Press, 2003. 73–82. Print.

Gilbert-Rolfe, Jeremy. "Blankness as a Signifier." *Critical Inquiry* 24.1 (1997): 159–75. Print.

Gins, Madeline. *Word Rain*. New York: Grossman, 1969. Print.

Ginsberg, Allen. *Journals Mid-Fifties: 1954–1958*. New York: Harper Perennial, 1996. Print.

———. "Allen Ginsberg." Interview with Gary Pacernick. *American Poetry Review*. 26.4 (1997): 23–28. Print.

Gleason, Paul. "If It Could Be Wrapped." *EBR* 2004. 25 August 2005. Web. 8 August 2007.

Grice, Helena. "Placing the Korean American Subject: Theresa Hak Kyung Cha's *Dictee*." *Representing Lives*. Pauline Polkey and Alison Donnell, eds. London: Macmillan, 2000. 43–52. Print.

Gromala, Diane J and Yacov Sharir. "Dancing with the Virtual Dervish: Virtual Bodies." *Immersed in Technology: Art and Virtual Environments*. Anne Moser, ed. Boston: MIT Press, 1996. 281–286. Print.

Guerlac, Suzanne. "'Recognition' by a Woman!: A Reading of Bataille's *L'Erotisme*." *Yale French Studies* 78 (1990): 90–105. Print.

Hadfield, Gordon. "Sounding Time: Temporality, Typography, and Technology in Twentieth-Century American Poetry." Diss. State University of New York at Buffalo, 2005. Ann Arbor: UMI, 2005. AAT 3174131. Print.

Halpern, Tal Read. *Digital Nature: The Case Collection version 2.0*. 2002. Web.

———. "'Shots from the Obscure.' An Interview with Tal Halpern by Patrick F. Walter." 2003. Web. 22 June 2011.

Hansen, Mark. *New Philosophy for New Media*. Cambridge: MIT Press, 2006. Print.

Hantke, Steffen. *Conspiracy and Paranoia in Contemporary American Literature: The Works of Don DeLillo and Joseph McElroy*. Frankfurt: European Studies Peter Lang, 1994. Print.

Haraway, Donna. *Simians, Cyborgs and Women: The Reinvention of Nature*. New York: Routledge, 1991. Print.

Harwood, Graham. "Rehearsal of Memory." n.d. Web. 20 June 2011.

Hayles, Katherine N. "Bodies of Texts, Bodies of Subjects: Metaphoric Networks in New Media." *Memory Bytes: History, Technology, and Digital Culture*. Lauren Rabinovitz and Abraham Geil, eds. Durham: Duke UP, 2004. 257–82.

———. *How We Became Posthuman: Virtual Bodies in Cybernetics, Literature, and Informatics*. Chicago: U of Chicago P, 1999. Print.

———. *My Mother Was a Computer: Digital Subjects and Literary Texts*. Chicago: U of Chicago P, 2005. Print.

———. *Writing Machines*. Cambridge: MIT Press, 2002. Print.

Hejinian, Lyn. *The Language Inquiry*. Berkley: U of California P, 2000. Print.

Hix, H. L. *Understanding William Gass*. Columbia: U of South Carolina P, 2002. Print.

Howe, Susan. *The Birth-Mark: Unsettling the Wilderness in American Literary History*. Middletown: Wesleyan UP, 1993. Print.

———. "The End of Art." *Archives of American Art Journal* 14. 4 (1974): 2–7. Print.

Hutcheon, Linda. *A Poetics of Postmodernism: History, Theory, Fiction*. London and New York: Routledge, 1998. Print.

Huyssen, Andreas. *After the Great Divide: Modernism, Mass Culture, Postmodernism*. Bloomington: Indiana UP, 1986. Print.

Jackson, Shelley. *Patchwork Girl*. Watertown, MA: Eastgate Systems, 1995. CD-ROM.

Jacobus, Mary. *Women Writing and Writing about Women*. The Oxford Women's Series. London: Croom Helm, 1979. Print.

Jameson, Fredric. *Postmodernism: or, the Cultural Logic of Late Capitalism*. Durham: Duke UP, 1991.

Joyce, Michael. *Twelve Blue*. Eastgate Hypertext Reading Room, 1996. Web. 5 April 2012.

———. *Was*. Tuscaloosa: FC2, 2007. Print.

Kac, Eduardo. "Art at the Biobotic Frontier." n.d.Web. 20 June 2011.

Kang, Hyun Yi. "The 'LiberatoryVoice' of Theresa Hak Kyung Cha's *Dictee*." Elaine Kim and Norma Alarcon, eds. *Writing Self, Writing Nation*. Berkeley: Third Woman Press, 1994. 73–102. Print.

Kaplan, Caren, Norma Alarcón, and Minoo Moallem, eds. *Between Woman and Nation: Nationalisms, Transnational Feminisms, and the State*. Durham and London: Duke UP, 1999. Print.

Karl, R. Frederick. *American Fictions 1940–1980*. New York: Harper and Row, 1983. Print.

Kim, Elaine. "Poised on the In-Between: A Korean American's Reflections on Theresa Hak Kyung Cha's *Dictee*." Elaine Kim and Norma Alarcon, eds. *Writing Self, Writing Nation*. Berkeley: Third Woman Press, 1994. 3–30. Print.

———, and Norma Alarcon, eds. *Writing Self, Writing Nation*. Berkeley: Third Woman Press, 1994. Print.

Kirschenbaum, Matthew. *Mechanisms: New Media and the Forensic Imagination*. Cambridge: MIT Press, 2008. Print.

Kristeva, Julia. "Phonetics, Phonology and Impulsional Bases." Trans. Caren Greenberg. *Diacritics* 4:3 (1974): 33–37. Print.

———. *La révolution du langage poétique*. Paris: Editions du Seuil, 1974. Print.

———. *Revolution in Poetic Language*. Trans. Margaret Waller. New York: Columbia UP, 1984. Print.

Kuehl, John. *Alternate Worlds: A Study of Postmodern Antirealistic American Fiction*. New York: New York UP, 1989. Print.

Lecercle, Jean-Jacques. *Philosophy through the Looking-Glass: Language, Nonsense, Desire*. LaSalle, IL: Open Court, 1985. Print.

Leclair, Thomas. *The Art of Excess*. Urbana: U of Illinois P, 1989. Print.

Lee, Kun Jong. "Rewriting Hesiod, Revisioning Korea: Theresa Hak Kyung Cha's *Dictee* as a Subversive Hesiodic Catalogue of Women." *College Literature* 33.3 (2006): 77–99. Print.

Lee, Sue-Im. "Suspicious Characters: Realism, Asian American Identity, and Theresa Hak Kyung Cha's *Dictee.*" *Journal of Narrative Theory* 32:2 (2002): 227–58. Print.

Lewallen, Constance. "Theresa Hak Kyung Cha. Here Time and Place." *The Dream of an Audience*. Berkley: U of California P, 2001. 1–14. Print.

Lionnet, Françoise and Shu-Mei Shih, eds. *Minor Transnationalism*. Durham and London: Duke UP, 2005. Print.

Literary Saloon: The Literary Weblog. 17 Dec. 2003. Web. 4 March 2008.

Liu, Warren Tswun-Hwa. "The Object of Experiment: Figurations of Subjectivities in Asian American Experimental Literature." Diss. University of California at Berkley, 2004. Ann Arbor: UMI, 2004. AAT 3165471. Print.

Lowe, Lisa. "Unfaithful to the Original: The Subject of *Dictee.*" Elaine Kim and Norma Alarcon, eds. *Writing Self, Writing Nation*. Berkeley: Third Woman Press, 1994. 35–69. Print.

MacKendrick, Karmen. *Word Made Skin: Figuring Language at the Surface of Flesh*. New York: Fordham UP, 2004. Print.

Mallarmé, Stéphane. *Un coup de dés jamais n'abolira le hazard*. Paris: Editions de la Nouvelle Revue Française, 1914. Print.

Maltby, Paul. *Dissident Postmodernists: Barthelme, Coover, Pynchon*. Philadelphia: U of Pennsylvania P, 1991. Print.

Marcus, Ben. *The Age of Wire and String*. Normal, IL: Dalkey Archive Press, 1998. Print.

Marks, Laura. *The Skin of the Film: Intercultural Cinema, Embodiment, and the Senses*. Durham: Duke UP, 2000. Print.

———. *Touch. Sensuous Theory and Multisensory Media*. Minneapolis and London: U of Minnesota P, 2002. Print.

Markson, David. *Reader's Block*. Normal, IL: Dalkey Archive Press, 1996. Print.

Martone, Michael. *Michael Martone*. Tallahassee: FC2, 2005. Print.

Maso, Carole. *AVA*. Normal, IL: Dalkey Archive Press, 1993. Print.

———. *Break Every Rule: Essays on Language, Longing, and Moments of Desire*. Washington, DC: Counterpoint Press, 2000. Print.

———. "A Correspondence with Carole Maso." *The Salt Hill Journal* 8 (1999): 107–13. Print.

———. "An Interview with Carol Maso." *Barcelona Review* 20. Sept.–Oct. 2000. Web. 24 Nov. 2005.

———. "An Interview with Carol Maso." *Rain Taxi. Review of Books* 2.4 (1997–98). Web. 24 Nov. 2005.

———. Personal interview. 6 June 2006.

Massumi, Brian. *Parables for the Virtual: Movement, Affect, Sensation*. Durham, NC: Duke UP, 2002. Print.

McElroy, Joseph. "Joseph McElroy." Author's home page. n.d. Web. 4 March 2008.

———. "Midcourse Corrections." *The Review of Contemporary Fiction* 10.1 (1990): 9–56. Print.

———. "Neural Neighbourhoods and Other Concrete Abstracts." *TriQuarterly* 34 (1975): 201–17. Print.

———. Personal interview. 5 June 2006.

———. *Plus*. New York: Knopf, 1977. Print.

———. "Plus *Light*." 2002. TS. Bookmarks Future Letture Conference in Potenza, Italy, 25 May 2002.

———. "Socrates on the Beach. Thought and Thing." *Substances, Revue Française d'Etudes Américaines* 93 (2002): 7–20. Print.

———. "'Some Bridge of Meaning': A Conversational Interview with Joseph McElroy." Marc Chénetier, Antoine Cazé, and Flore Chevaillier. *Sources* 11 (2001): 7–38. Print.

Michaels, Walter Benn. *The Shape of the Signifier: 1967 to the End of History*. Princeton, NJ: Princeton UP, 2004. Print.

Min, Eun Kyung. "Reading the Figure of Dictation in Theresa Hak Kyung Cha's *Dictee*." Sandra Kumamoto Stanley, ed. *Other Sisterhoods: Literary Theory and U.S. Women of Color*. Urbana and Chicago: U of Illinois P, 1998. 310–24. Print.

Mitchell, W. J. T. *Picture Theory*. Chicago: U of Chicago P, 1994. Print.

Mix, Deborah. "Re-writing the Wor(1)d: Experimental Writing by Contemporary American Women (Toni Morrison, Betsy Warland, Theresa Hak Kyung Cha, Lyn Hejinian, Daphne Marlatt)." Diss. Purdue University, 1998. Ann Arbor: UMI, 1998. AAT 9900235. Print.

Moe, Carol. "Cross Cultural Intervention in Twentieth Century American Literary Theory: Another Look at *Dictee, The Bonesetter's Daughter, Dreaming in Cuban, So Far From God,* and *Song of Solomon*." Diss. University of California, 2004. Ann Arbor: UMI, 2004. AAT 3141967. Print.

Moi, Toril. *Sexual/Textual Politics: Feminist Literary Theory*. London and New York: Methuen, 1985. Print.

Moraru, Christian. *Rewriting: Postmodern Narrative and Cultural Critique in the Age of Cloning*. Albany: SUNY P, 2001. Print.

"New England Biolabs." n.d.Web. http://www.neb.com/nebecomm/default.asp. 20 Feb. 2008.

Oh, Stella. "The Enunciation of the Tenth Muse in Theresa Hak Kyung Cha's *Dictee*." *Literature Interpretation Theory* 13.1 (2002): 1–20. Print.

Oliver, Kelly. *Reading Kristeva. Unraveling the Double-Bind*. Bloomington and Indianapolis: Indiana UP, 1983. Print.

Olsen, Lance. *10:01*. Iowa Review Web 7.2. 2005. Web. 5 April 2011.

———. *Head in Flames*. Portland: Chiasmus Press, 2009. Print.

———. "Notes Toward the Musicality of Creative Disjunction, Or: Fiction by Collage." *Symplokē* 12.1–2 (2004): 132–33. Print.

———. "Talking with Lance Olsen. Interview with Flore Chevaillier." *Rampike* 20.1 (2011): 50–60. Print.

Olson, Charles. *Collected Prose*. Donald Allen and Benjamin Friedlander, eds. Berkley: U of California P, 1997. Print.

"Operon." n.d. Web. 20 Feb. 2008. https://www.operon.com/country.php?goto=/index.php.

Osborne, Karen Lee. "'The Blessed Syncope of Supreme Moments': The Music of Time in *AVA*." *AVA* CASEBOOK. n.d.Web.19 August 2007.

Ott, Brian L. "(Re)locating Pleasure in Media Studies: Toward an Erotics of Reading." *Communication and Critical/Cultural Studies* 1.2 (2004): 194–212. Print.

———. "Television as Lover, Part I: Writing Dirty Theory." *Cultural Studies = Critical Methodologies* 7.1 (2007): 26–47. Print.

Page, Barbara. "Women Writers and the Restive Text: Feminism, Experimental Writing and Hypertext." *Postmodern Culture* 6.2 (January 1996). Web. 19 August 2007.

Park, Josephine Nock-Hee. "'What of the Partition': *Dictee*'s Boundaries and the American Epic." *Contemporary Literature* 46.2 (2005): 213–42. Print.

Paul, Christiane. *Digital Art*. London: Thames & Hudson World of Art, 2003. Print.

Pérez, Emily. "The Hybrid and the Helix: A Journey into the Body/Text of *VAS*." *Gulf Coast: A Journal of Literature and Fine Arts*. Spring 2005. Web. 20 Feb. 2008.

Porush, David. *The Soft Machine: Cybernetic Fiction*. New York: Methuen, 1985. Print.

Poynor, Rick. "Evolutionary Tales." *Eye* 49. Web. 20 Feb. 2008.

Proietti, Salvatore. "Joseph McElroy's Cyborg Plus." *EBR* 18 Aug. 2004. Web. 27 Nov. 2007.

Proust, Marcel. *The Captive. Remembrance of Things Past*. Vol III. Trans. C. K. Scott Moncrieff, Terence Kilmartin, and Andreas Mayor. New York: Vintage Books, 1981. Print.

———. *La prisonnière*. Paris: Gallimard. 1985. Print.

Re, Margaret. "Reading Matthew Carter's Letters." *Typography Speaking: The Art of Matthew Carter*. Margaret Re, ed. New York: Princeton Architectural Press, 2003. 13–30. Print.

Reed, Ishmael. *Mumbo Jumbo*. New York: Simon & Schuster, 1972. Print.

Roudiez, Leon. Introduction. *Revolution in Poetic Language*. Julia Kristeva. New York: Columbia UP, 1984. 1–10. Print.

Russell, Charles. "Individual Voice in the Collective Discourse: Literary Innovation in Postmodern American Fiction." *Sub-stance* 27 (1980): 29–39. Print.

Scalapino, Leslie. *Dahlia's Iris—Secret Autobiography + Fiction*. Tallahassee: FC2, 2003. Print.

Scherr, Rebecca. "Syn/aesthetics: Touch, Sound, and Vision in the Works of Gertrude Stein, Djuna Barnes, and Muriel Rukeyser." Diss. University of Minnesota, 2005. Ann Arbor: UMI, 2005. AAT 3156794. Print.

Schneiderman, Davis. "Notes from the Middleground: On Ben Marcus, Jonathan Franzen, and the Contemporary Fiction Combine." *EBR* 2006. Web. 20 Feb. 2008.

Shiach, Morag. *Hélène Cixous: A Politics of Writing*. London and New York: Routledge, 1991. Print.

Shih, Shu-Mei. "Nationalism and Korean American Women's Writing. Theresa Hak Kyung Cha's *Dictee*." *Speaking the Other Self. American Women Writers*. Jeanne Campbell Reesman, ed. Athens and London: U of Georgia P, 1997. 144–64. Print.

Siegel, Lee. *Love in a Dead Language*. Chicago: U of Chicago P, 1999. Print.

Silbergleid, Robin. "'Treblinka, A Rather Musical Word': Carole Maso's Post-Holocaust Narrative." *MFS Modern Fiction Studies* 53.1 (Spring 2007): 1–26. Print.

Silliman, Ron. *The New Sentence*. Berkley: Roof Books, 2003. Print.

Sontag, Susan. "Against Interpretation." *Against Interpretation and Other Essays*. New York: Farrar, Strauss and Giroux, 1966. 4–14. Print.

———. "The Pornographic Imagination." *Styles of Radical Will*. London: Secker and Warburg, 1969. 35–74. Print.

Sorrentino, Gilbert. *Mulligan Stew.* Normal, IL: Dalkey Archive P, 1996. Print.

Spahr, Juliana. "Postmodernism, readers, and Theresa Hak Kyung Cha's *Dictee* ([De] Colonizing Reading/[Dis]Covering the Other)." *College Literature* 23.3 (1996): 23–44. Print.

———. "'Tertium Quid Neither One Thing Nor the Other' Theresa Hak Kyung Cha's *DICTEE* and the Decolonization of Reading." *Connective Reading and Collective Identity.* Juliana Spahr, ed. Tuscaloosa and London: U of Alabama P, 2001. 119–52. Print.

Spivak, Gayatri Chakravorty. *In Other Worlds: Essays in Cultural Politics.* New York and London: Metheun, 1987. Print.

Stevick, Philip. *Anti-Story: An Anthology of Experimental Fiction.* Glencoe: Free Press, 1971. Print.

Still, Judith. "Horror in Kristeva and Bataille: Sex and Violence." *Paragraph* 20.3 (1997): 221–39. Print.

"Stratagene." n.d. Web. 20 Feb. 2008. http://www.stratagene.com/homepage/.

Sukenick, Ronald. *In Form: Digressions on the Act of Fiction.* Carbondale: Southern Illinois UP, 1985. Print.

———. *Long Talking Bad Condition Blues.* New York: Fiction Collective, 1979. Print.

———. *Narralogues: Truth in Fiction.* Albany: SUNY P, 2000. Print.

———. "The New Tradition in Fiction." *Surfiction.* Raymond Federman, ed. Chicago: Shallow Press, 1981. 35–45. Print.

———. "Unwriting." *American Book Review* 13.5 (1992): 4, 26–27. Print.

Suleiman, Susan Rubin. "Pornography, Transgression, and the Avant-Garde: Bataille's *Story of the Eye.*" *The Poetics of Gender.* Nancy K. Miller, ed. New York: Columbia UP, 1986. 117–36. Print.

Surkis, Judith. "Georges Bataille: An Occasion for Misunderstanding." *Diacritics* 26.2 (1996): 18–30. Print.

Tabbi, Joseph. *Postmodern Sublime. Technology and American Writing from Mailer to Cyberpunk.* Ithaca: Cornell UP, 1996. Print.

Tambornino, John. *The Corporeal Turn: Passion, Necessity, Politics.* Plymouth: Rowman and Littlefield Publishers, 2002. Print.

Tanner, Tony. *Scenes of Nature, Signs of Men.* Cambridge and New York: Cambridge UP, 1987. Print.

Tenhaaf, Nell. "Mysteries of the Bioapparatus." *Immersed in Technology: Art and Virtual Environments.* Anne Moser, ed. Boston: MIT Press, 1996. Print.

Thacker, Eugene. "Review of *VAS.*" *Leonardo* 39.2 (2006): 166. Print.

Tomasula, Steve. "Multimedia Writing." n.d. Web. 18 Feb. 2006.

———. "Narrative + Image = Two Languages (in One Work) x Multiple Meanings [A Rationale for an Issue]." ebr7 image + narrative, part two summer 98.Web. 18 February 2006.

———. Personal correspondence. 19 Oct 2006.

———. Personal interview. 29 March 2006.

———. "Steve Tomasula." Author's home page. n.d. Web. 20 Feb. 2008.

———. *VAS: An Opera in Flatland.* Art and design by Stephen Farrell. Chicago: U of Chicago P, 2004. Print.

———. *TOC.* Tuscaloosa: FC2, 2009. CD-ROM.

Twelbeck, Kristen. "'Elle venait de loin'—Re-reading *DICTEE*." *Holding Their Own: Perspectives on the Multi-Ethnic Literatures of the United States*. Dorothea Fischer-Hornung and Raphael-Hernandez Heike, eds. Tübingen, Germany: Stauffenburg, 2000. 227–40. Print.

Utterback, Camille. Personal Website. n.d. Web. 20 June 2011.

———. *Text Rain*, 1999. Art Installation.

Vanderborg, Susan. "Of 'men and mutations': The Art of Reproductions in Flatland." *The Journal of Artists' Books* 24 (Fall 2008): 4–11. Print.

Wilson, William S. "Fields in the Novels of Joseph McElroy." *EBR* 3, 1995. Web. 12 Nov. 2007.

Wong Sunn, Shelley. "Unnaming the Same: Theresa Hak Kyung Cha's *DICTEE*." *Feminist Measures. Sounding in Poetry and Theory*. Lynn Keller and Cristanne Miller, eds. Ann Arbor: U of Michigan P, 1997. 43–68. Print.

Yuknavitch, Lidia. *Real to Reel*. Tallahassee: FC2, 2003. Print.

index